AFRICAN AMERICAN FOLKTALES

Recent Titles in
Stories from the American Mosaic

Native American Folktales
Thomas A. Green

AFRICAN AMERICAN FOLKTALES

Edited by
Thomas A. Green

Stories from the American Mosaic

GREENWOOD PRESS
Westport, Connecticut • London

Library of Congress Cataloging-in-Publication Data

African American folktales / edited by Thomas A. Green.
   p. cm. — (Stories from the American mosaic)
Includes bibliographical references and index.
   ISBN 978–0–313–36295–8 (alk. paper)
1. African Americans—Folklore. 2. Tales—United States. 3. United States—Folklore.
I. Green, Thomas A., 1944–
GR111.A47A37   2009
398.2'0896073—dc22   2008037863

British Library Cataloguing in Publication Data is available.

Library of Congress Catalog Card Number: 2008037863
ISBN: 978–0–313–36295–8

First published in 2009

Greenwood Press, 88 Post Road West, Westport, CT 06881
An imprint of Greenwood Publishing Group, Inc.
www.greenwood.com

Printed in the United States of America

∞

The paper used in this book complies with the
Permanent Paper Standard issued by the National
Information Standards Organization (Z39.48–1984).

10 9 8 7 6 5 4 3 2 1

Contents

Preface

African American Folktales is designed to provide educators, students, and general readers with examples of a range of traditional African American narrative types: fictional tales, legends, myths, and personal experience narratives. Moreover, the examples in this anthology attempt to represent the cultural diversity within African America. Because of the popularity of Joel Chandler Harris's *Uncle Remus Tales,* the popular image of African American narrative is the animal fable presented in the southern dialect as rendered by Harris and European American authors who followed the principles he established. In reality, the subject matter ranges from animal fable to the romantic fairy tale, levels of diction from the colloquial to the formal, and language forms from the Africanized English Gullah of the southern coast to French Creole. As noted in the body of this work, the folktales are informed by African, European, and Native American traditions—traditions that, in turn, were impacted by the resulting African American art forms. The tales reflect the environment, cultural adaptations, and prevailing concerns of the respective areas from which they are drawn, as well as more general features of the African American experience. The introductions to each tale comment on these issues. The concluding general bibliography provides additional resources for those readers who wish to explore these issues in greater depth.

The collection is divided into four sections. "Origins" encompasses those narratives that focus on beginnings and transformations: the creation of the world and its inhabitants, how animal species acquired their physical characteristics, and how the family came to be here, for example. "Heroes, Heroines, Villains, and Fools" presents a cross-section of major character types that populate African American folktales. "Society and Conflict" contains considerations of social issues ranging from conventional morality and intergroup conflicts to the common experience of bondage that many, but by no means all, African American families shared. Finally, "The Supernatural" concentrates on traditional tales of the dead, the magical, and the monstrous.

The narratives have been modified from their original forms for the benefit of contemporary readers. The modifications have been held to the minimum necessary to translate these tales for their intended audiences or to eliminate redundancy in some cases, and, in a few cases, alternative terminology has been substituted for terms (particularly racially charged terms) that would prove offensive to contemporary readers. The source of each selection is noted at its conclusion for the benefit of readers who wish to read the original texts.

ORIGINS

How Jackal Became an Outcast

The following narrative is said to have been brought directly from Africa. In it, Jackal plays the role of a trickster who uses his superior wit to manipulate Lion by appealing first to the stronger animal's vanity and later to his gullibility. Jackal, however, does not temper his wit with morality. This flaw leads to disaster both for the Jackal of this tale and for his descendants forever after.

The Jackal and the Lion were hunting in the jungle. "Brother Lion," said the Jackal, "the young elephant we seek is a good distance away. Well, it is not so far away either, but you see it will run around and around and in and out, and that will make the distance long. I see that you have a sore foot, and so long a journey might cost you your life. It would be a pity to lose your great head and pretty voice."

"It would, indeed," said the Lion. "I am glad to find someone who understands my worth."

"You see, Brother Lion," said the Jackal, "if I should get lost or killed the world would not miss me, but you, Brother Lion, you!"

"Yes, Brother Jackal," broke in the Lion, "my place could not be filled; but do not take my greatness too seriously. You are worth a little, and that little should be saved."

"Brother Lion" continued the Jackal, "I would gladly give my whole self for your pleasure. You lie down here in the shade, keep cool and think great thoughts, while I take your spear and run down and kill the elephant that you have long desired to eat. When I have done so I will return and take you to it!"

"Very good," said the Lion. "You are kind and thoughtful. Take my spear and best wishes and be off. I can almost taste the feast now."

The Jackal took the spear, and in a short time had killed the elephant and covered the body with leaves. It then ran to another road, cut its finger and let the blood drip here and there for a great distance. Then it returned to the Lion and said: "Brother Lion, I almost lost my life in killing the elephant. Just go through yonder forest until you come to the straight road. By the elephant's blood you can trace it to the spot where it fell. As soon as I rest

I'll be with you. I charge you now that to taste the meat before I come will mean death to you. This is a new law of the jungle."

The Lion went in search of the bloody path, and the Jackal returned to the elephant and began to eat. Now it happened that the Lion hurt his foot and, while binding it up, saw the Jackal eating and looking around.

When the Lion came up to the Jackal he said, "You little rascal, I have a notion to eat you for deceiving me."

"Be patient, Brother Lion; I am doing you a favor. Unless a Jackal eats of a young elephant first, its meat will kill a Lion. This is a new law of the jungle, and I am still in love with your great head and pretty voice. You remember I gave you a charge to this end."

"Yes," said the Lion, "I remember, and I thank you for saving my head and voice; but since you have tested the meat, what keeps me from eating my fill?"

Just another new law of the jungle," said the Jackal. "This new law says that such meat must be put upon a high stone tower where the sun's rays may strike it. Then all may eat it unharmed."

"Oh, Brother Jackal," said the Lion, "how can I ever pay you for saving my head and voice?"

"In this way," replied the Jackal. "According to the law, my wife and children must be masons upon the wall, and you and yours must hand up the stones; and you see there are plenty of them about here. Of course, I remain on the ground to direct. I have told my wife and children, and they are coming. You go and bring yours."

"That suits me quite well," said the Lion. "I'll be back with mine in a short while."

When the Lion and his family had returned, the Jackal and his family had eaten half of the elephant and were dancing. "You little rascal!" roared the Lion, "have you deceived me again?"

"Not a bit of it," replied the Jackal. "See that little bird lying dead there? That is the messenger of the new laws. By accident I killed it. The new law requires that the one who kills such a bird, and his family, must eat half the meat present as a punishment; and such a punishment as it has been! But for this new dance my wife invented we should all be dead. This means that you would be dead, too. The life of the Jackal in such a case goes into the bird. It becomes ten times as powerful as a Lion and kills everyone it meets. See?"

"I do," replied the Lion, "and thanks again for my head and voice. Let me remind you, Brother Jackal, that my wife and family are not likely to die at present from overeating."

"Let me remind you, Brother Lion, that one more speech like that from you will put life into that bird, and you will never eat another dinner."

"Thanks, Brother Jackal, for your wisdom and kindness. Let's build the tower."

In a short time the tower was erected. "How are we to get the meat up?" asked the Lion.

"Oh," said the Jackal, "my wife, who invented the dance, has invented a rope to pull the meat up with."

"I am glad to hear that, Brother Jackal," said the Lion, "for my wife, who is rather dull, may learn many things from yours."

"Brother Lion," said the Jackal, "when a Lion passes a compliment like that upon a Jackal's wife he had better roar it far and wide, or he will be counted a flatterer, and flattery puts life into that little bird."

The Lion roared the compliment until every beast in the jungle heard it. The Jackal's wife and children let down the rope and pulled the meat up.

"Brother Lion, there is one precaution we must take. That little bird lying there must never be allowed to come back to life, and there is but one way to do it."

"Brother Jackal, pray what is that?"

"Pick up that rock lying there by the bird. When my wife has pulled me to the top of the tower, throw it to me. If I catch it, the bird is dead forever. We will then pull you and your family up, and what a feasting there will be!"

"My dear Brother Jackal," roared the Lion, "you are all wisdom. Now you are up, and I am ready with the rock. Shall I throw it?"

"My dear Brother Lion," said the Jackal, "I am so high up I fear I shall not be able to catch it. There is one way to keep me from missing it. Put your wife right under my hands as I hold them out."

"She is there," called the Lion. "Now catch the rock." The Lion threw up the rock. The Jackal withdrew his hands, and it came back, striking the Lion's wife and almost killing her.

"You've killed Ma! you've killed Ma!" cried all the little Lions, and scampered off into the forest.

"That was a terrible mistake, Brother Lion," said the Jackal. "It was all your fault. You didn't ask me whether or not I was ready. That bird is coming to life! I feel it. Unless I can get you up here in five minutes it will be on wing and right after you. Now throw up the rock. That's right. I have it. Good for you. Here, wife, heat this rock and hand it back to me when I ask for it. You understand?"

"Yes, Mrs. Jackal," called the Lion, "hand your husband the rock when he asks for it, for that is indeed a precious rock."

The Jackal let down the rope, telling the Lion to tie it tightly around his body below the forearms. When this was done the Jackal began to pull the Lion up.

"Brother Lion," called the Jackal, "that little bird down there is moving."

"Sister Jackal," cried the Lion, "have you the rock?"

By this time the Jackal's wife was holding the rock with a pair of tongs, for it was very hot.

"That's right," shouted the Lion, "hold that rock carefully."

"That terrible bird!" mourned the Jackal.

"Ha, ha!" said the Jackal's wife, "I'll drop this hot rock into your mouth, and then how you'll kick and claw the air!" She tried to drop the rock, but the tongs would not open. She then tried to drop both tongs and rock, but could not. The tongs soon began to burn her hands. In trying to throw them from her, she fell from the tower and killed herself.

The Jackal dropped the rope and so freed the Lion. The tower trembled and fell. The little bird that the Jackal thought dead was the cause of the change. It was the spirit of the jungle and believed in fair play. It sang a sad song while the wife of the Jackal was being buried. It then sang joyously while the Lion and his wife and children, who had come back, ate the rest of the meat.

The Jackal was badly hurt and crippled by falling with the tower, yet he had to wait on the Lion and his family while they were feasting. And ever afterwards the Jackal was an outcast among animals, despised by all because of his evil and deceitful spirit.

Source: Adapted from "The Jackal and the Lion." Joseph Cotter, *Negro Tales* (New York: The Cosmopolitan Press, 1912), pp. 102–109.

Terrapin's Magic Dipper and Whip

The storyteller from whom this tale was collected in the 1920s was reported to have been born in West Africa and brought to Alabama as a slave. Tortoise, localized as Terrapin in the following tale, is among the most popular folktale characters in the narratives of the region. The plot in which a magical object provides an apparently unlimited food supply and another object dispenses beatings is likely to be European in origin. Therefore, the following explanation of the origin of Terrapin's shell and furtive behavior suggests the creative merging of two folk traditions: African and European.

It was famine time and Terrapin had six children. Eagle hid behind a cloud, and he went across the ocean and went to get the palm oil; he got the seed to feed his children with it. Terrapin sees it, says, "Hold on, it's a hard time. I got six children; can't you show me where you get all that food?"

Eagle says, "No, I had to fly across the ocean to get there."

Terrapin says, "Well, give me some you wings and I'll go with you."

Eagle says, "Alright. When shall we go?"

Terrapin says, "Tomorrow morning by the first cock crow." So tomorrow came, but Terrapin come in from Eagle's house says, "Cuckoo-cuckoo-coo."

Eagle says, "Oh, you go home. Lay down. It ain't day yet."

But he kept on, "Cuckoo, cuckoo, coo," and bless the Lord, Eagle got out, says, "What you do now?"

Terrapin says, "You put three wing feathers on this side of my body and three on the other, so I can fly across the ocean with you."

Eagle pull out six feathers and put three on one side and three on the other. Says, "Fly, let's see."

So Terrapin commence to fly. One of the wing feathers falls out. But Terrapin said, "That's all right, I got the other wings. Let's go." So they flew and flew; but when they got over the ocean all the eagle wing feathers fell out. Terrapin was about to fall in the water. Eagle went out and catch him. Put him under his wings. Terrapin says, "I don't like this."

Eagle says, "Why so?"

Terrapin says, "Gee, it stinks here." Eagle let him drop in the ocean. So he went down, down, down, to the underworld.

The king of the underworld meet him. He says, "Why you come here? What you doing here?"

Terrapin says, "King, we're in terrible condition on the earth. We can't get nothing to eat. I got six children and I can't get nothing to eat for them. Eagle he only got three and he go across the ocean and get all the food he need. Please give me something so I can feed my children." King says, "Alright, alright," so he goes and gives Terrapin a dipper. He says to Terrapin, "Take this dipper. When you want food for your children say:

> Bakon coleh Bakon cawbey
> Bakon cawhubo' lebe lebe."

So Terrapin carried it home and go to the children. He says to them, "Come here." When they all come he says:

> Bakon coleh Bakon cawbey
> Bakon cawhubo' lebe lebe.

Gravy, meat, biscuit, everything in the dipper. Children got plenty now. So one time he say to the children, "Come here. This will make my fortune. I'll sell this to the king." So he showed de dipper to the king. He says:

> Bakon coleh Bakon cawbey
> Bakon cawhubo' lebe lebe.

They got something. He feed everybody. Pretty soon everybody eating. So they ate and ate, everything, meats, fruits, and all like that. So he took his dipper and went back home. He says, "Come, children." He try to feed his children; nothing came. So Terrapin says, "Aw right, I'm going back to the King of the Underworld and get him to fix this up."

So he went down to the underworld and says to the king, "King, what's the matter? I can't feed my children no more."

So the king says to him, "You take this cow hide whip and when you want something you say:

> Sheet noun n-jacko
> nou o quaako.

So Terrapin went off and he came to cross roads. Then he said the magic:

> Sheet n oun n-jacko
> nou o quaako.

The cowhide whip commences to beat him. It beat, beat.

Cowhide said, "Drop, drop." So Terrapin drop and the cowhide stop beating. So he went home. He called his children in. He gives them the cowhide whip and tells them what to say, then he went out.

The children say:

> Sheet n-oun n-jacko
> nou o quaako.

The cowhide whip beat de children. It say, "Drop, drop." Two children dead and de others sick.

So Terrapin says, "I will go to the king." He calls the king, he call all the people. All the people came. So before he has the cowhide whip beat, he has an armor made and gets in there and gets all covered up.

Then the king say:

> Sheet n oun
> n-jacko
> nou o quaako.

So the cowhide whip beat, beat. It beat everybody, beat the king too. That cowhide whip beat, beat, beat right through the armor that Terrapin was wearing and beat marks on his back, and that's why you never find Terrapin in a clean place, only under leaves or a log. He's always hiding from that cowhide whip.

Source: Adapted from "Negro Folk Tales from the South (Alabama, Mississippi, Louisiana)," Arthur Huff Fauset. *Journal of American Folklore* 40(1927): 213–303, pp. 215–217.

Why Dogs Always Chase Rabbits

This animal tale offers an elaborate explanation for the reason dogs chase rabbits. In this case Rabbit's powers as a conjure man (practitioner of folk magic) bring him more attention than he intends. Along the way the tale presents stereotypes of European Americans and Native Americans, the two major ethnic groups with whom African Americans were compelled to compete in the southern United States.

In the good old times, Old Rabbit wasn't bothered any by the neighbors. It was miles to the corner of any one of his fields.

After awhile, Mister Indian and his folks set them up a settlement, but that ain't nothing, because Indian folks in those days was always roaming around and picking up their baggage and moving it here and yonder.

By and by, though, the white men came along a-chopping down the trees and a-digging up the earth. Then all the critters packed their Sunday-go-to-meeting clothes in their pillow cases and get ready to move, because they know that Mister White Man came for to stay, and he ain't one of the kind that wants to be crowded. That is all of 'em except Old Rabbit and the Squirrel family set out. They two allowed they were going to tough it out a while longer.

What pestered Old Rabbit more than all the rest was that white man's dog. It wasn't like the Indian dogs. It was one of them sharp-nosed hound-dogs that hunt all day and howl all night. It was as still as a fox on a turkey-hunt from the morning until candlelight, but just wait until the sun goes down and the moon comes up, and oh Lord! "Ah, oo-oo-oo-wow, ow, ow! Ah oo-oo-oo, wow, ow, ow! Ah oo-oooo, wow, ow, ow!" You could hear it go from almost sundown to almost sunup, and that was the most aggravating sound that God ever put in the throat of a living critter. It distracted Old Rabbit. He flounced around in the bed like a catfish on the hook. He groaned and he grunted, and he turned and rolled, and he just can't get no good rest.

Old Miss Rabbit she obliged to roll the bed-covers around her ears, she that scandalized.

"Why don't you get out of the bed and turn your shoe with the bottom-side up and set your bare foot onto it?" she say. "That would make any dog stop he yowling."

"Well! Ain't I done it forty-eleven time?" say Old Man Rabbit just foaming at the mouth like a mad dog and snorting like a bull. "Ain't I been hopping in and out the bed all the live-long night ? Because it stops that yowling for a half a jiff and then it tunes up again before I just kin get the bed warm under me."

"Ah oo-oo-oo, wow, ow, ow! Ah oo-oo-oo, wow, ow, OW! That old hound fetch a yowl that far make the man in the moon blink."

"Cuss that old dog! Cuss him say I! Why don't that old fool that owns him stuff a corncob down his throat, or chop him into sausage meat?" says Old Rabbit, says he. "I giving up on the sleeping question tonight," says he, "but I'll see to it that I ain't disturbed like this in my rest tomorrow," says he.

With that he bounces out on the floor and hauls on his britches and lights a candle, and he takes that candle in he hand, and he go poking around amongst the shadows like he's a-hunting for something.

Scratch, scratch! Scuffle, scuffle! He goes in the corners of the cupboard.

"Ah oo-oo-oo! wow, ow, ow!" goes the hound outside.

Scratch, scratch! scuffle, scuffle! Ah oo-oo-oo! Wow, ow, ow! Scratch, scratch! scuffle, scuffle Ah oo-oo-oo! Wow, ow, ow!

And so they keep it up, until old Miss Rabbit is as mad at one as the other.

"What are you doing, Mister Rabbit?" she says again and again, but Old Rabbit ain't about to satisfy her curiosity about that.

Directly, though, when he gets through and blows out the candle and the day is going to break, she starts noticing that he steps sorta lopsided.

"What is the matter, Mister Rabbit?" she ask. "Did you run a brier into your foot?"

"No," says he, mighty short, "I ain't got no brier in my foot that I know of."

At that she let fly a swarm of questions, but he just grins dry and says, "Ask me no questions and I tell you no lies. Don't bother me, old woman. I ain't feeling very strong in the head this morning, and I might have to answer questions with my fist if I get pestered."

That shut her up, in due course, and she set in to getting breakfast. Pretty soon she hollered out, "Who been touching the bread? Somebody been cutting the bread! I vow I've got to trounce greedy children for that. It appears like I can't set down nothing these days, but they've got to mess in it! I'm going to cut me a big hickory limb this mornin' And see of I can't lick some manners into the whole kit and caboodle of them!"

"No you ain't," says Old Rabbit, says he. "Just leave them young 'uns of mine alone. They ain't done nothing. I cut that bread, and I got that bread, and I ain't going to eat it up."

Pretty soon old Miss Rabbit sang out again. "Who's been cutting the bacon fat?" says she "and cutting it crooked too," says she. "I'm just going to leave the breakfast and set out and get that limb right now," says she.

"No, you won't," says Old Rabbit, says he. "I ain't going to have the sense beat out of them young 'uns of mine. I took that fat and I got that fat, and if I cut the slice crooked that's my look out," says he. "I paid for it, and I'm going to cut it with the saw or the scissor if I feel like it," says he.

With that he gets up and walks off, lim-petty-limp.

Miss Rabbit ain't seen no more of him until sundown. Then he come in looking mighty tuckered out, but just a-grinning like a baked skunk. He set down he did, and ate like he been hollow clear down to his toes, but he won't say nothing. When he got through he sort of stretched himself and said, "I'm going to go to bed. I got a heap of sleep to make up, and I bet no dog ain't going to disturb my rest this night."

And they don't. They wasn't a sound, and Miss Rabbit made a great admiration at that in her mind, but she ain't got nobody to talk it over with until the next morning, when Old Rabbit get up as happy and sassy as a yearling. Then he had the big tale to tell, and this was what he told her.

When he was a-fooling in the cupboard he get him a piece of bread, and he tied that bread on his foot. Then he cut him a slice of bacon, and he put that on top of the bread. Then he slipped on his shoe and he started out. He did that because he was going to fix him some shoe bread for feed to that dog, because if you wear bread in your shoe and then give it to a dog, and he eats it, that dog yours. He's going to follow you to the ends of the Earth, that he is. The bacon he put against that bread give it a good taste, and to fool the folks that see him, because he was going to let on like he run a brier in he foot and took and put that bacon on the wound to draw out the soreness and keep him from a-getting the lockjaw.

Well, he tromped around until the white man went to the field, and then he sort of slipped up easy-like, and he flung that shoebread in front of that old hound dog. It gulped it down in just one swallow. You know them hound dogs just always been hungry since the minute they was born, and you can't fill him up no more than if they got holes in him the same as a colander.

The minute that shoebread had been swallowed, that old hound dog just naturally longed after Old Rabbit. He took out after him through the brush so swift that it sort of scared Old Rabbit. He was just a-studying about a-leading that hound to the creek, and a-tying a rock around his neck and a-drowning him, but this here terrible hurry surprised him so that he just ran like the Old Devil was a-trying to catch him. Here they had it! Up hill and down hollow, across the field and around the stump, over and under, around and around, catch if you can and follow if you can't. Oh sirs, that was a race!

No telling how it might have come out of Old Rab hadn't run across an Indian man with a bow and arrow.

The Indian began to fit the arrow to the string for to shoot that Rabbit, when he hollered out loud as he could holler for the shortness of his breath, "Oh! hold on, Mister Indian Man, hold on a minute. I'm a-fetching you a present," says he, "a mighty nice present," says he.

"What you fetch?" says the Indian Man, kind of suspicious-like.

"It's a dog," says Old Rabbit, a-working his ears and a-flinching his nose, because he heard that dog a-crackling through the brush, a mighty nice fat dog, Mister Injun Man. I hear tell that your old woman was feeling poorly, and I was a-bringing this here hound dog so you could make a stew out of him," says he. "I'd a-fetched him ready cook," says he, "but my old woman just nowhere as good as yours in the making of stews," says he. "I was planning on fetching a string of onions for seasoning, but then I don't know of you like your dog stew with onions," says he.

The Indian certainly was tickled with that idea, but he don't say much. He just sort of grunted and looked towards the brush.

"That's him! That's my hound dog a-coming!" said Old Rabbit a-flinching more and more as the crackling came nearer. "You better shoot him, just as he bounces out of the brush, because that's a monstrous shy dog, monstrous shy! He won't follow nobody but me, and I can't go along home with you and take him, because I'm lame. Last night I couldn't sleep my left behind foot hurt so, and now I got him tied up in bacon fat. Shoot him right here, Mister Indian! That the best and the safest thing to do, come on!"

Just that minute out jump the dog, and — zim! Mister Indian just shot him and pinned him to the ground.

Then Old Man Rabbit mopped the sweat off his face and loped off home, at least that's the tale he told the family, and if it ain't true nobody ain't a-denying it these days, and as he say to he old woman, bit a good laughing tale today, but it was monstrous solemn yesterday.

Since that time all the hound dogs is surely bewitched, because of they catch a glimpse of a rabbit tail out they take out after it.

Source: Adapted from "Ol' Rabbit an' the Dawg He Stole," Mary A. Owen. *Journal of American Folklore* 9 (1890): 135–138.

Why Frog Has No Tail

*In the following folktale, Frog incurs Wolf's wrath and loses his tail
due to the antics of Rabbit. Rabbit displays the trickster's common
trait of conquering a stronger character by deceit, but landing in trouble because he cannot resist taunting his dupe. Caught up in the
conflict, Frog becomes the innocent victim of Rabbit's guile and Wolf's
frustration.*

Once upon a time there was a rabbit and a wolf, and the rabbit and the
wolf was working for a man. They were driving oxen. So the wolf and rabbit
decided to steal one. The wolf had children and the rabbit didn't.

So they stole the ox and they killed it. They skinned it and they cleaned it.
Then they cut it into four parts; that was to get it out of the way quick.
When they got it killed Rabbit asked Wolf what would he do if some ladies
came and asked him for some meat. Wolf said he wouldn't do anything, he'd
just give the ladies some. Old Rabbit told Wolf to stay till he came back.

The rabbit borrowed four suits and the rabbit come back all dressed up as
a lady and asked the wolf would he sell her a piece of meat. The wolf said,
"Oh no, lady, I'll give you a piece," as he gave her a hind quarter.

The rabbit went back and dressed again and when he come back he asked
for another hind quarter. But the wolf didn't known she carried that on her
back.

Rabbit came back. He asked the wolf to sell some meat. He give the rabbit
a full quarter. He went back home and dressed again and asked to sell some
meat for her supper. Then he went back home and stored it all.

He came back as a man from work. He said to Wolf, "Oh, Mr. Wolf,
where's all the meat?"

Wolf said, "Oh, man, some ladies called to buy, and I give them the meat
and there is nothing left but the head and the guts. You take the head and I'll
take the guts."

So the next day Wolf goes by the rabbit's house. Rabbit saw him comin'
and got his fiddle and began to play:

Folly-rolly day,

You eat the meat and I eat the guts,
Folly-rolly day,
You eat the meat and I eat the guts,
Folly-rolly day.

And the wolf asked Rabbit to play it again. When he understood that Rabbit was taunting him over the trick he had pulled, Wolf began to run the rabbit. He chased him until he reached a hollow tree. When they reached the tree Rabbit ran into the hollow part. The wolf couldn't get him out. He saw a frog and asked the frog to watch the tree until he came back.

Frog said, "What for?" He told him the rabbit was up there and if he get the rabbit he would kill him and give the frog one half.

Wolf went home and got his ax. He would cut the tree down; limb by limb he would split it.

The rabbit was up in the hollow tree. He pretended as if he was eating. The frog heard him. The frog asked him what he was eating.

Rabbit said, "Oh, man, good things!" He asked Frog did he want some of it.

Frog said, "Yes." The rabbit told him to look up in the tree. He filled the frog's eyes full of pepper, and the frog had to get the pepper out of his eyes. Rabbit got away. When the wolf couldn't find the rabbit in the tree, he asked the frog had he been away. The frog told him no, he hadn't closed his eyes and neither had he been away. Frog began to edge away from Wolf to get close to the water, and when the frog began to leap the wolf cut the frog's tail off with his ax, and the frog been bumping when he travels ever since and hasn't had no tail.

Source: Adapted from "Negro Folk Tales from the South (Alabama, Mississippi, Louisiana)," Arthur Huff Fauset. *Journal of American Folklore* 40(1927): 213–303, pp. 233–234.

Grandfather's Escape to Free Haven

In this family saga, the narrator provides historical details of her ancestors' origins in Africa, bondage in Maryland, and escape from enslavement. Tales of this sort serve to create bonds among people sharing a common experience whether the experience is based on kinship, ethnic heritage, or historical events.

As a child I remember hearing the old folks telling me of their terrible life which they led on the large farms of Maryland before the Emancipation.

My grandfather had been a chieftain's son [in Africa], and he remembered the time when he was a little fellow, playing with some other boys on the banks of the sea, and a band of men swooped down on them and carried them from their own people. My grandfather remembered the heavy gold bracelets and armlets of his rank and those slave-stealers took the gold ornaments from him.

My grandfather had a black mark about an inch wide running down his forehead to the tip of his nose. This mark was the sign of his tribe. He was tall and very much respected by the other slaves and the slaveholder down in Maryland. He married, raised a family and grew old. Even in his old age he was a valuable piece of property, but soon he became useless in the fields and his master agreed to give him his freedom.

But the old man, my grandfather, asked for the freedom of his youngest son, who was my father. This the master refused to do at first but at the earnest insistence of my grandfather, he agreed...upon condition that the son, who was a great swimmer and diver, should dive into the Chesapeake Bay where a ship had sunk years before with a load of iron. If the son were successful in bringing to the surface this load of iron, then my grandfather and his son, my father, should go free.

My grandfather tied a rope around my father's waist and for over three months the two of them brought the pieces of iron to the shore for old master. They say that sometimes the son stayed under the water so long that my grandfather had to drag him up from the wreck and lay him on the ground and work over him like you'd work over a drowned person.

Day after day the two worked hard and finally there wasn't no more iron down there and they told the master so and he came down to the wreck and found out they was telling the truth...but still he wouldn't let them go. The old man, yes, but not the son who was handy around the place, an' everything.

But my grandfather kept asking for his son and the old master said that if the two of them brought up the sound timbers of the old wreck, then he would keep his word and let them go. So my grandfather and his son, my father, between them brought up all the sound timber that was part of the wreck. It was cheaper to get this wood and iron from the wreck than to buy it, so the master wanted it.

The wreck had stayed down on the bottom of the Chesapeake Bay for over twenty years but nobody except my father had been able to dive that deep. So you see it was just like trading off some of the young slaves on the farm to be able to get the iron and wood. When the two finished that chore, and it was a mighty big chore, too, they went up to the big house and asked for their freedom.

The master sent them back to their cabin and said that since the old man wasn't no good any more, and it just cost the master money to feed him, he could go whenever he pleased, but the son was going to stay on the farm and if he tried any foolishness, he would sell him south. Selling a slave south meant that the slave would be taken to one of the slave trader's jails and put on the block and be sold to some plantation way down south. And no worser thing could happen. Many a family was separated like that, mothers from their children, fathers from their children, wives from their husbands, and the old folks say that a pretty girl fetched (brought) a higher price and didn't have to work in the fields. These young girls, with no one to protect them, were used by their masters and bore children for them. These white masters were the ones who didn't respect our women and all the mixing up today in the south is the result of this power the law gave over our women.

Well, when the old man and his son knew it was no use, that their master did not intend to let them go, they began to plot an escape. They knew of the Underground Railroad, they knew that if they could get to Baltimore, they would meet friends who would see them to Philadelphia and there the Friends (Quakers) would either let them settle there or send them to other people who would get them safely over the border into Canada.

Well, one night my grandfather and my father made up their minds and my grandfather could read and write so he wrote hisself out a pass. Any slave who went off the farm had to have a pass signed by the master or he would be picked up by a sheriff and put in jail and be whipped.

So my grandfather had this pass and got safely through to Baltimore. There they hid for several days and waited for an agent of the Underground Railroad.

One night they were dressed in some calico homespun like a woman and rode to Philadelphia on the back seat of a wagon loaded with fish. In Philadelphia, the town was being searched by slaveholders looking for runaway slaves, so the people where they were supposed to stay in Philadelphia hurried them across the river about ten miles.

My grandfather and my father stayed across the Delaware from Philadelphia, helping a farmer harvest his crops, and they built a cabin and soon other escaped slaves from among their former neighbors slipped into New Jersey where they were.

Finally there was almost a hundred escaped slaves in the one spot and because they were free at last and this place was a haven just like the Bible talked about, they decided to stay there and so they got together and called the place Free Haven.

My uncle says that he reached there by hiding in the woods all day and walking at night. So many people came from Maryland that they changed the name of the little village to Snow Hill, which was the name of the town nearest the farms from which all or most of the people had run away. The post office people made them change the name again and now it is Lawnside, but I was born there sixty-four years ago and I still think of it as Free Haven.

Source: "Interview of Mary Thomas, American Life Histories: Manuscripts from the Federal Writers' Project," 1936–1940. Levi C. Hubert. Ms. Div., Lib. of Congress. *American Memory*. Lib. of Congress, Washington. October 12, 2005. http:// memory.loc.gov/ammem/wpaintro/wpahome.html.

The Little Finger

"The Little Finger" offers a legend of one family's African roots.
Within the legend is embedded a variation of a plot known interna-
tionally as "The Singing Bone" in which the spirit of a murder victim
calls out for justice through a bone, other remains, or an instrument
made from the victim's body. Beyond the account of Manga's experi-
ences as a slave in Africa and the explanation for her coming to Loui-
siana, the narrative reveals that no race or culture has a monopoly on
cruelty and inhumanity.

Before we came here, poor devils, we were all free, we were not obliged to
work for any master. It is the whites who came into our country, Africa, to
get us. They stole some of us; they bought some of us from our fathers for
a red handkerchief, for a bottle of tafia (cheap rum), or an old gun. When
we went to war those who were caught were sold to the whites who came
to trade on the seacoast. We were led away, tied together, tied two by two,
and when we reached the seacoast like a herd of cattle, men, women, and
children, we were exchanged, not for money, but for any kind of merchan-
dise, and the whites put us into ships and brought us here. This is how we
became slaves in America.

When Manga, my grandmother, arrived at the seacoast, she saw a pretty
little town with small houses. There were many ships, and they seemed to
be dancing on the sea; some were going up, others down. It was the wind,
you know, that was blowing and shaking up the sea. My poor grandmother,
who was young then, was afraid when she saw they were putting all the
Negroes on board the ships. She thought they were going to drown them
in the sea. A white man came to her and bought her from her master.
He took her to his house and told her in her own language, "I bought you
to take care of my little boy." He had a pretty house with a store in it, and
a pretty garden. Behind the house was an orange grove, and the trees were
so large that there was a fine shade underneath. To show you how my grandmother's country was a good one, I will tell you that the orange were in
bloom the whole year; there were flowers and little oranges and ripe oranges
all the time.

The house was near the sea, and every mornimg Manga took little Florimond to take a bath. The little boy was so pretty and his father and mother
were so good, that Manga would not have left them for anything in the
world. She loved little Florimond so much; his hair was curly and his eyes
were blue. His skin was white and rosy. Everybody adored the poor boy;
he was so pretty and smart. He could sing so well and imitate all birds so
admirably that often they thought it was the Nita that was singing in the
trees. Nita is a little bird in Africa which sings at night when the moon is
shining. It perches on the top of the tallest tree; and if there is a light breeze
it sings better, for the swinging of the branch helps the little bird to sing, as
the rocking of the hammock helps a man's lullaby. Florimond imitated the
Nita so well that everybody was mistaken, and it amused the boy very much.

Florimond's father used to trade with the people that lived far in the
woods, so one day he started to get gold dust and elephants' teeth. On leaving he said to Manga: "Take good care of my wife and my little boy. You
know I gave you already a pair of shoes; I will give you, on my return, a fine
dress and a necklace." The first time Manga put on her shoes they hurt her
so much that she could hardly walk. She took them off on arriving at the
house, and sat on the steps looking at her toes . "Wiggle, wiggle, poor
things," she said, "you were in prison just now you are free now, you are
glad, is it not? Oh! I shall never shut you up again. I don't understand how
white folks can put their toes in such things!" From that time Manga never
put shoes on.

Well, the master went into the big woods, and three days afterwards the
lady said to Manga to take Florimond to the sea and give him a bath. While
the little boy was playing with the shells and the white sand, they saw a skiff
with several persons come ashore. A white man disembarked, and passed by
Manga, and she felt a peculiar sensation, as if some misfortune was to happen.
The eyes of the man shone like those of a cat in the dark. As he passed, he said,
"Good morning, Florimond," but the little boy did not reply anything. When
they arrived home the lady sent them to play in the yard, and every time the
master was away the strange man would come to the house. Florimond did
not want to see him, and he said one day he would tell his father about the
stranger.

The latter said to Manga, "You little black imp, if ever you open your
mouth about what you see here, I will cut your tongue with my big knife then
I will carry you to my ship, sew you up in a sack, and throw you into the sea
for the fish to eat you." Manga was so frightened that she would not have
said a word even if they had whipped her for a whole day. In the evening
Florimond cried so much that it was with great difficulty that Manga
succeeded in putting him to sleep. Her cot was near the bed of the little
boy, and during the night she saw the pirate enter the room with a big stick.

He struck the little boy on the head and said, "He is dead. I will put him in
the hole which I dug in the yard. Now I must attend to the black girl."

Manga, however, had already run away into the yard, but the man, thinking that she was in the road, ran out to catch her. Florimond's mother came into the room, took the little boy's body in her arms, and buried him in a hole near the place where Manga was. She was not quite through with her ugly work when she heard a noise and ran away.

She met the man, who said: "I believe the girl has gone to the woods; we need not trouble about her any more; the lions and tigers will soon eat her up. Now I must go on board my ship, and when I come back I will take you with me."

The lady went into the house, and Manga came out of her hiding place. She felt so weak that she could hardly stand, but before she left she kissed the ground where her dear little master was buried. She said, "Farewell, little angel," and ran into the woods. She preferred to stay with the wild animals than with the cruel mother.

After walking for some time as fast as she could, she stopped by a bayou in the wood, drank some water, and sat down to rest. She fell asleep, but soon she was awakened by loud talking. She saw some men standing around her, and among them was her master, who seemed to be very angry, "What are you doing here so far from my house? I left you to take care of my little boy. I suppose you did something wrong and ran away." Manga did not reply anything, because she remembered the threats of the pirate. The master ordered his men to bring her back to his house, and he hastened to go home.

He found his wife, who was weeping bitterly, and she said to him, "Oh what a dreadful misfortune! Manga let Florimond fall on his head, and our poor little boy is dead. I wanted to kill her, but she ran away, and I don't know where she is. If ever I catch her I will strangle her with my own hands."

When the poor man heard that his dear boy was dead, he fell in a swoon. They put him in bed, and he remained fifteen days delirious. During that time the lady said to Manga that she would kill her if she opened her mouth. She shut the girl in a cabin, and gave her nothing but bread and water.

At last Florimond's father got out of bed, but he would not be consoled, and he wept all day for his little boy. As Manga was still in her prison, her master did not see her, and did not think of her. One day as he was walking about in the yard, he looked from time to time at his dear boy's grave, and tears flowed from his eyes. In the meantime the Nita was singing on a tree near by, and its song was so sad that the poor man felt more sad than ever. It seemed to him it was his Florimond who was singing, and he came to the grave and looked at it a long time. All at once the poor father thought he was dreaming. He saw something that was so strange that many people will not believe it, but so many people told me the same story, that I believe it is as sure as the sun is shining.

When the lady had buried the little boy, she had not had time to cover the body completely, and one little hand was out of the grave, and it was the pretty little finger which was moving as if it was making a sign to call some-one. The little finger moved on one side and then on the other, and never stopped beckoning, so to say. The poor father dug up the earth with his hand and uncovered the body. He found it as fresh as if it had just been buried, and he took it in his arms and carried it to the house. He put the boy on a bed and rubbed him so long that the child came back to consciousness.

The father sent for a surgeon, who began to attend to the boy, and said that he would revive. There was no danger for his life, as the skull was not broken; the child was only in a state of lethargy, and would soon be well again. Indeed, in a few days Florimond was running about as if nothing had happened, but he never said anything about his mother and the stranger, and the lady at last allowed Manga to leave her prison. Remorse had taken hold of Florimond's mother; she grew thinner every day, and one evening, in spite of the most tender care, she died.

Her last words were, "Oh! my God, forgive me!" She was buried in the grave where her little boy had been, and as to the pirate, he never came back. They say that he was hanged.

After his wife's death Florimond's father left Africa, and sold poor Manga. She was put upon a ship, and this is how she became a slave in Loui-siana, and related to me the story of the little finger.

Source: Adapted from "The Little Finger," Alcée Fortier. *Louisiana Folk-Tales* (Boston & New York: American Folk-Lore Society, 1895), pp. 75–81.

HEROES, HEROINES, VILLAINS, AND FOOLS

Rabbit Becomes King of the Frogs to Win a Wealthy Wife

Throughout wide areas of Africa, Tortoise, Hyena, and Hare shared the role of trickster. In the folklore of the American South, however, Rabbit assumed overwhelming popularity as the hero who survived by superior wit, and, in most cases, defeated socially superior and physically stronger characters through cunning schemes. On the other hand, as revealed in the following tale, his self-serving motives allowed little room for the consideration of the fates of minor characters who became pawns in his con games.

Mr. Rabbit was hard to please in love affairs. Those upon whom his eyes fell were either too ugly or too poor, and in some cases both. At last he concluded that the greatest failure in the world is courting that does not end in a wedding.

He arose early one morning and sat down by the roadside to think over the different flowers along the path of love that had proven thorns to his soul. As he sat there, taking them up and dismissing one by one, with a frown on his face and a bachelor-like sourness in his soul, he chanced to see a beautiful maiden tripping over the meadows. As soon as he saw that she was pretty, he believed he loved her, as soon as he learned that her father was rich, he knew it.

"O soul, my poor wounded soul ! A smile from yon creature of grace and beauty would cure you. Let us haste and secure the remedy. I can well afford to exchange a task like this for the smiles of so pretty a wife and her father's pocketbook."

Mr. Rabbit knew his only stock in trade was wit, so he sharpened this and visited the girl's father. He walked up to the old gentleman and said, "Good morning, sir. My name is Mr. Rabbit. I have come to be your son-in-law, and your daughter has my letter of introduction."

The old gentleman was so surprised at Mr. Rabbit's words he did not call his daughter to test their truthfulness. He admired his visitor's boldness and readiness of speech and, after talking awhile, invited him out to breakfast.

Having learned the girl's name during the conversation, Rabbit spoke to her on coming out, and also took her by the hand. Now, he carried in his hand a stamp bearing the words "I propose."

After breakfast the old gentleman asked his daughter if she had Mr. Rabbit's letter of introduction, and she answered by holding up her hand. Then he asked her if she had ever met him before, and she said she had not. Without further ado he seized Rabbit by the throat and said, "My dear child, this whole thing has been forced upon you. Now, how shall I punish the impudent young whelp?"

"Why, father," said she in her sweetest tones, "let both of us punish him by making him your son-in-law."

Seeing that he could not withstand the combined forces of Cupid, his only daughter, and a wily lover, the old gentleman said: "Well, Mr. Rabbit, you may have the girl on the condition that you go down to the great frog settlement and prove that you are master of all the frogs there. This must be done by tomorrow at twelve o'clock."

"It shall be done," said Mr. Rabbit.

He dressed himself as strangely as possible, and, taking a looking-glass in his hand, went down to the frog settlement. He stood by the branch and waved the glass until the frogs gathered around him.

"This is not the place," said he. "This is not the place."

"Yes, it is," said an old frog. "It is the very place that has been here all the time."

Mr. Rabbit looked again and said, "It is the place, sure enough."

"Didn't I tell you so?" said the old frog. "If this place had moved, we would have known it."

This served to open the conversation. While talking, Rabbit held the glass so the frogs could see themselves. He told them it was a soul-drawing machine, and that by looking into it the soul would come out of the body and go behind the glass.

"Do you know," said Rabbit, "why Mr. Snake swallows so many of you? It is simply to get your souls. As the soul is in the body, he must swallow the body, also. Let him see that the soul is out of the body, and he will no longer bother the body, but go after the soul. If the soul is behind the glass, he can't get it. So you see, gentlemen, every frog should have a glass. All he has to do is to carry the glass with him, and, when Mr. Snake comes, just hold it up so as to see himself. Mr. Snake, seeing the soul out of his reach, will scamper off."

All agreed with Rabbit, but wanted to know where glasses sufficient for all could be had.

"Ah," said Rabbit, "that is my business here. I have come to build a factory for making them. All you have to do is to turn the wheel I will make. This wheel will turn the mill and out will come the glasses. There will be no charges."

The frogs agreed to turn the wheel as long as needed. Then Rabbit built a watermill for grinding wheat and corn, and put the wheel above the water. The frogs knew no better.

"In order to turn the wheel," said Mr. Rabbit, "you frogs must be divided into as many bands as there are paddles to the wheel. The first band must jump upon a paddle and force it down, then jump into the water and swim to shore ready for the next turn. Each band must do so in turn, and the wheel will go roun.' There are several things you must do. You must not be seen until I give the signal. Then you must come, start the wheel, and keep it going until I tell you to stop. At the second signal you must bellow as loudly as you can, or your souls will be so long in getting behind the glass that Mr. Snake will catch them. On the third signal you must dance as you come around, or the glass will be easily broken."

All agreed, and said there should not be a single hitch in the program.

Then Rabbit sent for his father-in-law to come, and bring his wheat with him. He did so, but laughed at Rabbit's mill-wheel.

"The wheat will be ground," said Rabbit, approaching the water and giving the signal agreed upon with the frogs.

At the first signal the frogs came by hundreds and sent the wheel over and over again in great haste. At the second signal they began to bellow; and, at the third, to dance. This procedure was continued, and in a short time the wheat was all ground.

"Now," said Mr. Rabbit, "I am not a member of the family as yet, but see what a means of income I am. How will it be further on? By the way, my father-in-law-to-be, how do you like the wedding-march my slaves are playing for me?"

"Very well, my son Rabbit, very well," said the old gentleman. "Come, let us have the ceremony." They then proceeded to the magistrate, where Mr. Rabbit and the young lady were duly wedded.

What became of the mill? Mr. Rabbit cared nothing for a cheap affair like that when he had succeeded in securing a pretty wife and rich father-in-law.

What about the frogs? There is no telling how long they turned the wheel, bellowed, and danced; or how they got the glasses from between the millstones.

Source: Adapted from "How Mr. Rabbit Secures a Pretty Wife and a Rich Father-in-Law," Joseph Cotter. *Negro Tales* (New York: The Cosmopolitan Press, 1912), pp. 127–132.

Rabbit and Tar Man at the Well

The following folktale is without a doubt the most widely recognized narrative plot in African American traditional culture. "Br'er Rabbit and the Tar Baby" was first introduced to American popular culture by Joel Chandler Harris ("Uncle Remus") and later was brought to an even larger audience via the Disney motion picture Song of the South. *As the story of "Rabbit and Tar Man at the Well" demonstrates, the tale circulates orally in versions that are distinct from yet obviously related to the Harris and Disney versions.*

Once upon a time there was a water famine, and the ponds went dry and the creeks went dry and the rivers went dry, and there wasn't any water to be found anywhere, so all the animals in the forest met together to see what could be done about it. The lion and the bear and the wolf and the fox and the giraffe and the monkey and elephant, and even the rabbit, everybody who lived in the forest was there, and they all tried to think of some plan by which they could get water. At last they decided to dig a well, and everybody said he would help, all except the rabbit, who always was a lazy little rascal, and he said he wouldn't dig.

So the animals all said, "Very well, Mr. Rabbit, if you won't help dig this well, you shan't have one drop of water to drink."

But the rabbit just laughed and said, as smart as you please, "Never mind, you dig the well, and I'll get a drink all right."

Now the animals all worked very hard, all except the rabbit, and soon they had the well so deep that they struck water and they all got a drink and went away to their homes in the forest. But the very next morning what should they find but the rabbit's footprints in the mud at the mouth of the well, and they knew he had come in the night and stolen some water. So they all began to think how they could keep that lazy little rabbit from getting a drink, and they all talked and talked and talked, and after a while they decided that someone must watch the well, but no one seemed to want to stay up to do it.

Finally, the bear said, "I'll watch the well the first night. You just go to bed, and I'll show old Mr. Rabbit that he won't get any water while I'm around."

So all the animals went away and left him, and the bear sat down by the well. By and by the rabbit came out of the thicket on the hillside and there he saw the old bear guarding the well. At first he didn't know what to do. Then he sat down and began to sing:

Cha ra ra, will you, will you, can you?
Cha ra ra, will you, will you, can you?

Presently the old bear lifted up his head and looked around. "Where's all that pretty music coming from?" he said.

The rabbit kept on singing:

Cha ra ra, will you, will you, can you?
Cha ra ra, will you, will you, can you?

This time the bear got up on his hind feet.
The rabbit kept on singing:

Cha ra ra, will you, will you, can you?
Cha ra ra, will you, will you, can you?

Then the bear began to dance, and after a while he danced so far away that the rabbit wasn't afraid of him any longer, and so he climbed down into the well and got a drink and ran away into the thicket.

Now when the animals came the next morning and found the rabbit's footprints in the mud, they made all kinds of fun of old Mr. Bear. They said, "Mr. Bear, you are a fine person to watch a well. Why, even Mr. Rabbit can outwit you."

But the bear said, "The rabbit had nothing to do with it. I was sitting here wide-awake, when suddenly the most beautiful music came right down out of the sky. At least I think it came down out of the sky, for when I went to look for it, I could not find it, and it must have been while I was gone that Mr. Rabbit stole the water."

"Anyway," said the other animals, "we can't trust you any more. Mr. Monkey, you had better watch the well tonight, and mind you, you'd better be pretty careful or old Mr. Rabbit will fool you."

"I'd like to see him do it," said the monkey. "Just let him try." So the animals set the monkey to watch the well.

Presently it grew dark, and all the stars came out; and then the rabbit slipped out of the thicket and peeped over in the direction of the well. There he saw the monkey. Then he sat down on the hillside and began to sing:

Cha ra ra, will you, will you, can you?
Cha ra ra, will you, will you, can you?

Then the monkey peered down into the well. "It isn't the water," said he. The rabbit kept on singing:

> Cha ra ra, will you, will you, can you?
> Cha ra ra, will you, will you, can you?

This time the monkey looked into the sky. "It isn't the stars," said he. The rabbit kept on singing.

This time the monkey looked toward the forest. "It must be the leaves," said he. "Anyway, it's too good music to let go to waste." So he began to dance, and after a while he danced so far away that the rabbit wasn't afraid, so he climbed down into the well and got a drink and ran off into the thicket.

Well, the next morning, when all the animals came down and found the footprints again, you should have heard them talk to that monkey. They said, "Mr. Monkey, you are no better than Mr. Bear; neither of you is of any account. You can't catch a rabbit."

And the monkey said, "It wasn't old Mr. Rabbit's fault at all that I left the well. He had nothing to do with it. All at once the most beautiful music that you ever heard came out of the woods, and I went to see who was making it."

But the animals only laughed at him. Then they tried to get someone else to watch the well that night. No one would do it. So they thought and thought and thought about what to do next.

Finally the fox spoke up. "I'll tell you what let's do," said he. "Let's make a tar man and set him to watch the well."

"Let's do," said all the other animals together. So they worked the whole day long building a tar man and set him to watch the well.

That night the rabbit crept out of the thicket, and there he saw the tar man. So he sat down on the hillside and began to sing:

> Cha ra ra, will you, will you, can you?
> Cha ra ra, will you, will you, can you?

But the man never heard. The rabbit kept on singing:

> Cha ra ra, will you, will you, can you?
> Cha ra ra, will you, will you, can you?

But the tar man never heard a word.
The rabbit came a little closer:

> Cha ra ra, will you, will you, can you?
> Cha ra ra, will you, will you, can you?

The tar man never spoke.

The rabbit came a little closer yet:

> Cha ra ra, will you, will you, can you?
> Cha ra ra, will you, will you, can you?

The tar man never spoke a word.

The rabbit came up close to the tar man. "Look here," he said, "you get out of my way and let me down into that well." The tar man never moved. "If you don't get out of my way, I'll hit you with my fist," said the rabbit. The tar man never moved a finger. Then the rabbit raised his fist and struck the tar man as hard as he could, and his right fist stuck tight in the tar. "Now you let go of my fist or I'll hit you with my other fist," said the rabbit. The tar man never budged. Then the rabbit struck him with his left fist, and his left fist stuck tight in the tar. "Now you let go of my fists or I'll kick you with my foot," said the rabbit. The tar man never budged an inch. Then the rabbit kicked him with his right foot, and his right foot stuck tight in the tar. "Now you let go of my foot or I'll kick you with my other foot," said the rabbit. The tar man never stirred. Then the rabbit kicked him with his left foot, and his left foot stuck tight in the tar. "Now you let me go or I'll butt you with my head," said the rabbit. And he butted him with his head, and there he was; and there the other animals found him the next morning.

Well, you should have heard those animals laugh. "Oh, ho, Mr. Rabbit," they said, "now we'll see whether you steal any more of our water or not. We're going to lay you across a log and cut your head off."

"Oh, please do," said the rabbit. "I've always wanted to have my head cut off. I'd rather die that way than any other way I know."

"Then we won't do it," said the other animals. "We are not going to kill you any way you like. We are going to shoot you."

"That's better," said the rabbit. "If I had just stopped to think, I'd have asked you to do that in the first place. Please shoot me."

"No, we'll not shoot you," said the other animals; and then they had to think and think for a long time.

"I'll tell you what we'll do," said the bear. "We'll put you into a cupboard and let you eat and eat and eat until you are as fat as butter, and then we'll throw you up into the air and let you come down and burst."

"Oh, please don't!" said the rabbit. "I never wanted to die that way. Just do anything else, but please don't burst me."

"Then that's exactly what we'll do," said all the other animals together. So they put the rabbit into the cupboard and they fed him pie and cake and sugar, everything that was good; and by and by he got just as fat as butter.

And then they took him out on the hillside and the lion took a paw, and the fox took a paw, and the bear took a paw, and the monkey took a paw; and then they swung him back and forth, and back and forth, saying: "One for the money, two for the show, three to make ready, and four to go." And up they tossed him into the air, and he came down and lit on his feet and said:

> Yip, my name's Mr. Cotton-tail;
> Catch me if you can.

And off he ran into the thicket.

Source: Adapted from "The Rabbit That Wouldn't Help Dig a Well," John Harrington Cox. "Negro Tales from West Virginia," *Journal of American Folklore* 47 (1934): 341–357, pp. 342–347.

Compair Lapin and the Little Man of Tar

A comparison between the preceding narrative from West Virginia, "Rabbit and Tar Man at the Well" and the Louisiana Creole tale "Compair Lapin and the Little Man of Tar" illustrates the diversity that exists within the African American folktale repertoire. Although both tales are built around the same plot, the former develops in a rural setting and focuses on Rabbit's ability to entrance watchmen a musical spell. In contrast, the latter tale demonstrates that Lapin (Rabbit) is a charming, but deceitful, politician able to deceive the highest authority of the land and to woo the most desirable lady of the court. Originally recorded in French Creole, the level of diction also sets the following tale apart from versions commonly encountered in anthologies of African American folklore.

I am going to relate to you something which is very funny, as you are going to see, and which happened a long time ago.

When the animals had the earth for themselves and there were yet but few people, God ordered them not to eat each other, not to destroy each other, but said that they might eat the grass with all kinds of fruits that there were on the earth. That was better, because they were all His creatures and it pained Him when they killed each other; but as quickly as they would eat the grass and fruits, He, God, would take pleasure to make them grow again to please them. But they did not obey the Master! Mr. Lion began by eating sheep, the dogs ate rabbits, the serpents ate the little birds, the cats ate rats, the owls ate chickens. They began to eat each other, they would have destroyed each other, if God had not put a stop to all that! He sent a great drought to punish their cruelty. It was a thing which was funny, nevertheless, as you are going to see.

There was smoke in the air, as when they burn cotton stalks; it looked as if there was a light mist. After sunset, the heaven remained red like fire. The sea, the rivers, the lakes, all began to fall, to fall; all fell at the same time, until there was not a drop of water remaining. Neither did the dew fall early in the morning to moisten the grass. Ah! I tell you, my friends, all animals found themselves in a great trouble. They were roaming about everywhere; their tongues were hanging out; they became thin, thin.

There was among them a doctor who was called Dr. Monkey; he was half wizard, half voudou (voodoo). They said he knew a great deal, but he was a big talker, and did very little. He said to the other animals that it was because they had made so many sins that God sent them all these misfortunes to punish them; that if there were any among them who wanted to pay, he would pray to make the rain fall. He had already succeeded very often when he asked for something; God in heaven always listened to his prayer. There was also a famous thief there; it was Mr. Fox, who ate all the chickens there were in the neighborhood.

He said to the other animals, "Don't you listen to Dr. Monkey; he is a rascal; he will take your money without giving you anything for it. I know him, he is a rascal; you will have no rain at all! It is better that we should dig a well ourselves. We need not count upon anything else. Let us go! Hurrah! Right off, if you are all like me, for I am very thirsty."

Then Dr. Monkey told him, "I think indeed that you are hungry, you pirate; now that you have finished eating all the chickens there were here, you are coming to play the braggart here."

Mr. Fox told him, "You are a liar; you know very well that the owls, the polecats, and the weasels are eating all the chickens, and you come and say it is I. You know that if there is a thief here, it is you, you prayer merchant."

All the other animals, tigers, lions, wolves, elephants, crocodiles, serpents were running about to look for water. They had all assembled to hear the dispute of Dr. Monkey and Mr. Fox, and I must tell you that if a hog grunts, a dog barks, a wolf howls, a cow bellows, each kind of animal has its own language. A tiger or an elephant or a lion cannot speak the language of another animal. Each one speaks his own language, but when they are together, they all understand each other. The hog which grunts understands the dog which barks. It is not like us men; if a German comes to speak with a Frenchman or an American, he will not understand, any more than if an Englishman were to speak with a Spaniard who does not understand English. We men are obliged to learn the language of other nations, if we want to converse with them.

Animals are not at all like that; they understand each other as if they to spoke the same language. Well, I must tell you that Mr. Fox pretended that if there was such a drought, the rain not having fallen for a year, so that all the grass was parched up, and the trees had lost their leaves, and there were neither flowers nor fruits, it was because there were no clouds in the heaven to give water, and not a prayer could make the rain fall. "All the water has gone into the ground. We must dig a large well in order to have water to drink. Listen to me, my friends, and we shall find water."

Lion, who was the king, opened his mouth. He roared, the earth shook, he spoke so loud! He beat his sides with his tail, and it made a noise like a big drum in a circus. All the other animals lay flat on the ground. He said, "By the very thunder, the first fellow who will speak to me about prayers, I shall give him some thing which will make him know me. I am a good fellow; when did I ever eat another animal? It is a lie, and I say that the little lawyer Fox is a fine little fellow. He is right, we must dig a well to have water immediately. Come here, Compair Bourriquet (Donkey), it is you who have the finest voice here; when you speak, it is like a soldier's trumpet. You will go everywhere to notify all animals that I, the king, I say that they must come to dig up and scratch the earth, that we may have water. And those that don't want to work, you will report them. You will come right off that I may compel them to do their share of the work or pay some other animal to do it."

Bourriquet was so glad he was to act as a newspaper, that he began to bray so loud that it was enough to render anybody deaf.

"Depart, depart," said the king, "or I shall strike you."

Then Bourriquet reared, and thought he was doing something nice, he was so proud that the king had confidence in him, and then that gave him the opportunity to order the other animals to come, in the name of Lion, the king. On starting, he put down his head, then he kicked half a dozen times with both feet, and made a noise which was as if you were tearing up a piece of colonnade. That is his way of saluting the company, when he is glad.

Now, all the animals which he met, he told them, that if they did not come immediately to dig up and scratch the ground to make a well, surely King Lion would eat them up. They were all so much afraid, that they all came, except Compair Lapin, who was gnawing a little piece of dry grass.

"Don't listen to what I tell you, remain there, and don't come right off, you will see what the king will do with you."

"I don't care at all for you and the king together; come both of you, you will see how I'll fix you. You may go to the devil. Do I drink? Where did I ever use water? Surely, that is something new to me. You are a fool, donkey that you are, I never drink, a rabbit never drinks. My father and my grand-father did not know how to drink, and as I am a real rabbit, I don't use water. Go away, you big ears; for if I take my whip, I shall show you your road, and make you trot faster than you ever galloped in your life. If you knew me as I know you, you would not have stopped here."

Bourriquet saw that he could do nothing, so he went away, but he was not as proud as when he started to tell all animals that the king ordered them to come to work. As soon as he arrived near the king, he said, "Master, I went on all your errands, I saw all the animals in the world, only Compair Lapin does not want to listen to reason. He says he does not need water, let those who need it look for it. Besides, if you are not satisfied, he will make you trot. You have no right to command him, he is free, free as air; he has no master, none but God."

When the king heard that, he told Tiger, who was there, to go with the Bear to arrest Compair Lapin and bring him here. "Take care you don't eat him on the way, for if you do, I'll give you such a beating as you never had before. You hear? Well, go."

They started, and traveled a good while before they arrived. During this time, all the animals were working hard, each one had his share of the work, and they had even left a big piece as Compair Lapin's task and that of the two who had gone to arrest him. They looked everywhere: in the prairie, on the mountain; at last they fell on Compair Lapin, who was eating the root of a cocklebur which was full of water. You know that rabbits know how to dig up the earth and find water below, in the roots of plants.

At the same moment when they arrived near him, Compair Lapin was singing a little song which he had made about the king. He said in it that the king was a fool, and did not know how to govern, for his wife had many husbands, and he was laughing to himself, and that perhaps, after they finished to dig that well, the king would make all the animals pay taxes to drink the water from the well they had dug with their sweat. I am not so foolish, I am not going to work for that fellow! Let the others do it, if they are fools, I don't care any more for the king than a dog for Sunday. Tra la la.

The tiger approached without making any noise, and then he said: "Good morning, Compair Lapin, I ask your pardon, if I disturb you, but I don't do it on purpose; the king has ordered me to arrest you. I must obey him. You know that the weak must submit to the strong; this is why I advise you not to resist, because the Bear and I will be obliged to eat you. Take my advice, come quietly, perhaps you will come out all right. Your mouth is honeyed. You will get Mr. Fox to defend you; he is a good little lawyer and does not charge dear. Come, let us go."

When Compair Lapin saw that he could not do otherwise, he let the officers of the king arrest him. They put a rope around his neck, and they started. When they were near the dwelling of the king, they met Dr. Monkey on the way. He said: "Compair Lapin, I think you are a pupil of Mr. Fox. You will have to pay for it; you are gone up, my old fellow. How are you now? Don't you feel something getting cold within you? That will teach you to read the newspaper and meddle in politics on Sundays, instead of going quietly to mass!"

Compair Lapin answered briefly: "I don't care for anything you say, old Monkey! And then, you know, he who must die, must submit to his fate. Just hush up, you rascal You are trying to injure me, but perhaps you will be the loser. I have not given up all hope; perhaps, before long, you will be in trouble. Each one his chance, that is all I have to tell you."

At last they arrived at a big tree which had been thrown down by the wind, and where the king was seated. The Tiger and the Bear, the two officers who were leading Compair Lapin, said to the king, "Here is the fellow!"

"Haw! haw!" said the king, "we shall judge him immediately."

Mr. Fox came slyly behind Compair Lapin, and told him in his ears, "When they will ask you why you spoke badly of the king, say that it is not true, that it is Bourriquet who lied to do you harm. And then flatter the king very much, praise him and make him some presents, you will come out all right. If you do what I tell you, you will find it well for you. Otherwise, if you are foolish enough to say all there is in your heart, take care, you will come out all wrong. I assure you that the king will make hash with you."

"You need not be afraid, Mr. Fox, I know what I have to do. I thank you for your good advice; I am a lawyer myself."

Compair Lapin had suspected that they would come to arrest him; he had spoken so badly of the king and the government. It is for that he had put on his best coat, and a big gold chain around his neck. He had said to one of his neighbors with whom he was quite intimate, who was called Compair Bouki (Hyena), when the latter asked him where he was going so finely dressed, "Yes, Compair Bouki, I shall soon go to see the king; and as it is the coat that makes the man, this is why I dressed so well. It always produces a good effect on proud and foolish people."

When the king was ready to begin the case of Compair Lapin, he said to the policemen, "Bring the prisoner here to be judged."

Then Compair Lapin advanced, and said, "O Lion, my dear Master, you sent for me; here I am. What do you want?"

The Lion said, "I have to condemn you, because you are always slandering me, and besides, you don't want to work to dig the well, which we are making so all will have water to drink. Everybody is working except you, and when I sent Bourriquet to get you, you said to him that I was a scoundrel, and that you would whip me! You will know that if your back has tasted of the whip, I have never been whipped; even my late mother did not dare to touch me! What do you have to say? You rascal with the long ears hanging down. I suppose they are so long, because the hounds have chased you so often. Speak right off, or I shall mash you, like a too ripe persimmon."

Compair Lapin kept quite cool; he knew that all that was a big wind that would bring neither rain nor thunder. He rubbed his nose with both paws, then he shook his ears, he sneezed, and then he sat down and said, "The king is justice on earth, as God is just in his holy Paradise! Great king, you who are more brave than all of us together, you will hear the truth. When you sent Bourriquet to get me, he who is more of a donkey than all the donkeys in the world, when he came to my house, I was sick, I told him, "You will tell the king that I am very sorry that I cannot come now, but here is a fine gold chain, which you will present to the king for me, and you will tell him that I have forty twelve other animals to work in my place. Because that is too necessary a thing to get a well; it is life or death for us, and we cannot do without it. Tell him also that only a great king like him could have such an idea, and enough brains to save us all!' What do you think he answered me? He replied that he did not care about a gold chain, that he did not eat that. If I had given him a basket of corn or some hay, he would have eaten it, but as to the chain, perhaps the king would hitch him up to the plough with that same chain, and he would be sorry to have brought it. When he went away, he said to me: 'Go on, papa, I shall arrive before you, you will know that the ox which is ahead always drinks clear water!' I suppose he meant that he would speak before I should have the chance to be heard! As I want the king to believe that I am not telling stories, I have a witness who was there, who heard all our conversation. If the king will have the kindness to listen to his testimony, he will hear the same thing I have just told him." Compair Lapin bowed to the king, and put the gold chain around Lion's neck, and then he sat down on one side smiling, he was so sure that his gift would produce a good effect and help him to come out all right from his trouble.

Now, Lion said to Mr. Fox to speak quickly. "I know all that business, and if you come here to lie, I'll break your neck. You need not wag your tail and make such grimaces, as if you were eating ants. Come on, hurry! I have no time."

"Dear Master Lion," said the Fox, "I shall tell you how all that happened: Compair Lapin, whom you see here, is the best friend you have. The proof of it is that he brought a big chain to make you a present. You will never see a Bourriquet do that; that is sure, because there is not in the world a greater clown than those donkeys. Dan Rice took twenty-one years to train a donkey! He says that for $100,000 he would not undertake again such a job. He would prefer to train fifty twelve thousand Lions, because they would eat him up, or he would do something good with them. Well, I must tell you, Mr. Lion, you, who are the king of all animals, that same Bourriquet, whom you sent to represent you, came to lie on you, and as to Compair Lapin, his soul is as white as snow! Although Dr. Monkey has your confidence, it is he who is governing secretly and advising all your people, and putting them in rebellion against you, the king, to establish another government, where that same Dr. Monkey and Bourriquet will govern in your place, when they will succeed in putting you out. That is what they have been trying to do for a long time, and that is what Compair Lapin and I wanted to tell you."

When the king heard that, he said, "That is all right; I am glad you told me so. You can go with Compair Lapin, I acquit him."

But while they were hearing the case, Dr. Monkey and Bourriquet thought that it was not healthy for them to remain there, so they escaped when they saw that the wrong side was being warmed up; they vanished, and no one knew where they had gone, so well were they hidden. After that Compair Lapin and Mr. Fox both remained in the same parish where the king resided. Mr. Fox was his deputy or chief clerk, and the other was first mate; that is to say, he commanded the others and made them work to finish digging the well with their paws.

At last the well was completed! All the animals drank, and they became strong again. The lioness recovered her health also, and some time after that she gave birth to twelve little cubs as yellow as gold, and all as pretty as could be. The king was so glad that he pardoned all that were in the penitentiary, and he allowed the exiles to return. He granted their pardon. He told them all to go and drink the water of the well. Then you may imagine that Dr. Monkey with his accomplice Bourriquet came out of their hole to mingle with the others. But they began to spy and to watch all that was being done or said.

One day they met Mr. Fox who was speaking of the government affairs in order to increase the tax. He and Compair Lapin found that there was not enough money in the treasury for them to become rich quickly. When Dr. Monkey saw them both together, he began to smile. He came near them, he bowed and said: "Let us forget what has passed, we must not be looking for those old papers. Let us be friends and live quietly like good neighbors." You might have thought they were the best friends when they parted. Dr. Monkey said to his partner Bourriquet, "You see these two fellows Compair Lapin and Mr. Fox, they are scoundrels. I must get the best of them, or they will beat me; that is all I know!"

As Compair Lapin had said, when they judged him, that he never drank water, the king had told him, "Take care that you never try to drink water from this well; I want to see if you say the truth, and I order every one to watch you."

You will not believe me when I tell you that it is true that rabbits never drink water, there is always enough water for them in the grass which they eat. But expressly because they had forbidden Compair Lapin to drink from that well, he wished to do it. All the other animals praised that water so highly: it was so clear, so good. That gave him such a thirst, that he felt at every moment as if he had eaten well-peppered salt meat. He said to himself, "I don't care I shall drink, and I shall see who is going to prevent me. Besides, if they catch me, I shall always have the daughter of the king to protect me. She will find some way of preventing them from troubling me, for she has much influence with her father."

He did as he said; every evening he drank his fill. But at last he wanted to drink in the daytime also. It was a strange well. Its water was not like any other water. It made people drunk like whiskey. Only, instead of making you sick after you were drunk, it made you much stronger than before, and they were beginning to perceive that all those who were old were growing young again. Even the vegetables which you watered with it, if you cut them, the next day they would grow as fine as the day before.

When Compair Lapin began to see the effect of that water he said, "I must have some for the day also, it does me a great deal of good; and as I am much older than the daughter of the king, I must become as young as she. Let me be, I shall arrange it. Don't you say anything." Well, when it was dark, he took his little calabash, which contained about two bottles of water, he went to the well, and filled it up. But he was so careful that the guard, which they put every evening near the well, saw nothing.

Dr. Monkey and Bourriquet watched all the time, because they could not forget how Compair Lapin had treated them whilst he was being judged. Therefore, they had sworn that they would catch him. But in spite of all their efforts, they lost their trouble and their time. At last, one day, Dr. Monkey went to see Bourriquet, his comrade, and told him, "Come to my house, I have something to show to you." He showed him Ti Bonhomme Godron (a man made of tar), and said, "It is with that I want to catch the fellow; as this time I shall be able to prove that he is guilty, we shall have all his money, which the king will confiscate to give us for discovering all his rascalities."

They took Ti Bonhomme Godron; they put him in a little path where Compair Lapin was obliged to pass, very near the water, and then they left. They knew it was not necessary to watch; Ti Bonhomme Godron would attend to him without needing anybody's help.

I know not if Compair Lapin suspected something, but he came quite late that evening. He never came at the same hour, but he managed things so well that he always got his water, and no one could catch him. When he arrived the evening they had placed Bonhomme Godron there, he saw something black. He looked at it for a long time. He had never seen anything like that before! He went back home immediately and went to bed.

The next evening he came again, advanced a little closer, looked for a long time, and shook his head. At that moment, a frog jumped in the water. Compair Lapin flattened on the ground, as if crushed, and in two jumps he reached his house. He remained three days without returning, and Dr. Monkey and Bourriquet were beginning to despair, and to believe that it was true that Compair Lapin did not drink at all. But it was enough for this one that it was forbidden for him to be still more anxious to drink.

"Oh! well," said he; "I don't care! I have some money here, but the remainder is hidden in the briars. If they catch me, I shall pay the police, and they will let me go. Besides, I have the protection of the daughter of the king; every night, she comes to see me. It would be very strange if she did nothing for me. Besides, I have always instructed the police to let go a man who had money, and I suppose that they will make no exception for me, for they would lose the money which I would give them."

This reassured him. He started in the evening. It was a beautiful moonlight night, and everyone was out late promenading. It was the end of spring: the honeysuckle perfumed the air, the mockingbird was singing in the pecan tree, there was a light breeze, which caused the leaves of the trees to dance, and the rustle prevented anyone from hearing him walk. Everybody was in bed. Only the dogs, from time to time, were barking at the big clouds, which were fleeing before the wind.

"It is my turn now. I, Compair Lapin, I am going to drink, but a drink that will count." He took his calabash. When he arrived at the place where Bonhomme Godron was, the old fellow was still there. It had been warm during the day, and the tar was soft. When Compair Lapin arrived there, he said, "Hum, hum, you have been long enough in my way. I do not come to drink; that is a thing which I never do; I want to take a bath tonight; get away from here. You don't want to answer? I tell you that I want to take a bath, you black scoundrel."

Bonhomme Godron did not reply; that made Compair Lapin angry. He gave him a slap. His hand remained glued. "Let me go, or I shall strike you with the other hand." Bonhomme Godron did not reply.

He struck him with the other hand. It remained stuck also! "I'll kick you, you rascal, if you don't let me go." One foot remained stuck, and then the other one.

Then he said: "You are holding me that they might injure me, you want to try to rob me, but stop, you will see what I am going to do to you. Let me go, or I shall strike you with my head and break your mouth!" As he said that, he struck, and a mule could not hit harder, he was so mad. His head, however, my dear friends, remained stuck also. He was caught, well caught.

At daybreak, Dr. Monkey and Bourriquet arrived. When they saw Compair Lapin there, they laughed, they cursed him. They took a cart to bring him to prison, and all along the way they told the people how they had put a trap to catch the most famous rascal there was in the universe. It was the famous Compair Lapin who had so sullied the reputation of the king's daughter, that there was not a great prince who wanted to marry Miss Leonine, as Compair Lapin had spoken so much about his being her lover.

Mr. Fox, who was passing, heard all the bad things which Dr. Monkey and Bourriquet were saying about Compair Lapin, and he replied, "Yes, it is true, there is nothing like a thief to catch another thief."

When they were taking Compair Lapin to prison, all who passed on the road threw bricks at him, and they made a true clown of him. When he arrived in the presence of the king, the latter said to him, "Now, I would like to hear what you can say to get out of this scrape."

Compair Lapin replied, "When the tree falls, the goat climbs on it! I know I can die but once, I don't care. If it is my money they want, I assure you that they will never see it. When I was free, never Bourriquet and Dr. Monkey tried to quarrel with me; the wild hog knows on what tree he must rub himself. I assure you that they are famous rascals."

"You must not speak in that way before the king, but the king will try your case in a few minutes."

"What I say is well said; I am ready to hear the judgment."

After the king and his friends had consulted together, they found Compair Lapin guilty, and they condemned him to death. They ordered that he be put in prison until they could find an executioner willing to execute him. The king thought that he would get rid of a fellow who was too cunning for him, and also he would take vengeance on Compair Lapin, because he had injured Miss Leonine's character in such a manner that it was a scandal.

While Compair Lapin was in prison, he was thinking how he would manage to escape forever. He thought that he was in a worse plight than he had ever been in before. He said to himself, "By Jove! That is no child's play. I think that I am done for. Well, as I am tired, let me sleep a little. It will do me good." He lay down on the floor, and, soon after, he was snoring. He began to dream that the beautiful Leonine, the daughter of the king, was making a sign to him to tell him he need not be afraid, that she would fix everything all right.

He awoke contented, and at daybreak the jailer opened the door of his prison and said to him, "They have found an executioner willing to execute you, but before that, they must cut off your ears. It is Bourriquet who has offered his services to send you in the other world. Take courage, my old fellow. I am sorry for you. You are a good fellow, but you risked your life too often. You know that an ounce of prevention is better than a pound of cure; now it is too late. Good-bye, comrade." At the same moment the sheriff came with his deputies to take him to the place of execution.

They arrived at the steep bank of a little river. There were tall trees, grass, and briars everywhere. They chose a clear space. When they arrived, there was a big crowd: gentlemen, ladies, many children. All had come to see how they were going to kill Compair Lapin. The king was there with all his family. Miss Leonine, the daughter of the king, was there also. Oh but she was so beautiful with her curls, which shone like gold in the sun. She had a muslin dress as white as snow with a blue sash and a crown of roses on her head. The eyes of all were turned towards her; she was so pretty that they forgot completely Compair Lapin, who was trembling like a leaf.

Yes, indeed, he was sorry to leave such a large fortune and such a beautiful wife as the king's daughter. What pained him the most was to think that perhaps Dr. Monkey or Bourriquet would marry Miss Leonine as soon as he would be dead, because they both boasted that Compair Lapin was in their way. Without him, they said they would have succeeded long ago.

Now the king said, "Well, let us put an end to all this. Advance, Bourriquet, and read Compair Lapin his sentence." The king allowed him to choose his death, as he pleased: to be drowned in the river, burnt alive, or hung on a tree, or to have his neck cut with a sword.

"Yes, yes," said Compair Lapin, "all that at once, or one after the other, if that pleases you so much that I should die, well, I am very glad. Only, I was afraid that you would throw me in those great thorns, that would tear my skin and I would suffer too much, and then, the snakes and the wasps would sting me. Oh no, not that, not that at all! Tell the king to do all except throwing me in those briars; for the love of God, who is in Heaven, and who will judge you as you judge me!"

"Haw! Haw! You are afraid of the thorns? We want to see you suffer, suffer, you scoundrel."

They were making such a noise that the king said: "What is the matter?" He came closer, accompanied by his daughter, Miss Leonine, who had come to see if Compair Lapin was going to die bravely; that is to say, everyone thought so, but she had come to encourage him and reassure him, because she had sent word to him secretly, while he was in prison, that even if the rope was around his neck, she, Miss Leonine, would arrive in time to take it off and save him, because she loved him more than anything in the world.

They related to the king and to Miss Leonine what Compair Lapin had said, and how much afraid he was to be thrown in the thorns and to suffer.

Miss Leonine came forward and said: "Papa, I have a favor to ask you. I know that you hate Compair Lapin, and I also, because he has sullied my name. Well, I want to make you all see that what they said is not true. I want to see him suffer for all his stories; we must get rid of him, and I ask you to throw him in the briars and let him rot there; it is good enough for such a rascal."

All clapped their hands, they were so glad. "Throw him in the briars; it is there indeed we must throw him," said the king; "he must suffer. Quick! Hurry!"

They took Compair Lapin by each limb, they swung him once; poor devil, he was crying: "No, no, not in the briars, in fire, cut my neck, not in the briars."

They said: "Twice T'izp!" They threw him in a great bunch of thorns.

As Compair Lapin fell in his native country, he sat down, he rubbed his nose, shook his ears, and then he said: "Thank you, all of you; I thought you were stupid, but it is here my mother made me; I am at home here, and not one of you can come here to catch me. Good-bye, I know where I am going."

Miss Leonine also was very glad; she knew where she would meet Compair Lapin that very evening. That proves one thing to you, that Compair Lapin was a hypocrite and pleaded false things to know the truth. It proves another thing, that when a woman loves a man, she will do all he wishes, and the woman will do all in her power to save him, and in whatever place the man may be, the woman will go to meet him. This is why they say that what a woman wants, God wants also.

As I was there when all that happened, they sent me here to relate it to you. I have finished.

Source: Adapted from "The Tar Baby," Alcée Fortier. *Louisiana Folk-Tales* (Boston & New York, American Folk-Lore Society, 1895), pp. 39–53.

The Pitch Boy

This final example of the classic "Tar Baby" tale was found among the Natchez, one of the southern Native American cultures who welcomed African Americans to their ranks first as refugees from the system of bondage that existed in the South and later as valued members of the society . The following tale remains close to the standard plot found among other African American regional cultures , yet differs from the two previous narratives ("Rabbit and Tar Man at the Well" and "Compair Lapin and the Little Man of Tar") in some significant details. For example, Rabbit dons the skin of a gray squirrel to commit his theft. This shape-shifting motif is found in other tales of the Trickster Rabbit in Southern native America. While it is probably borrowed from the Natchez, changing shapes by changing skins is a common motif in African-influenced populations throughout the Americas.

All of the wild animals appointed a time to dig for water and when the time came assembled and began digging. But presently Rabbit gave up digging, and the others went on digging without him. They found water. Then they stationed two people to watch it. But Rabbit became very thirsty. He killed a gray squirrel, stripped off its hide, got into it, and came to the watchers. It was Rabbit who did it, but in the form of the gray squirrel he said that he had become very thirsty for lack of water. "You may drink water because you are just a gray squirrel," they said to him, and he drank. He drank all he wanted and went away. Then he pulled off the hide.

But when he thought of going back to drink again the hide had become hard and he could not got it on, so when he became thirsty he dipped up the water at night. But his neighbors came for a visit and when he set out water for his visitors they said to him, "Where did you find it?" and he answered, "I got it from the dew."

Then, following the tracks by the water, they saw signs of Rabbit, made an image of a person out of pitch and set it up near the place where they had dug the well.

The next night Rabbit came and stood there. "Who are you?" he said. There was no reply and he continued, "If you do not speak I will strike you." Rabbit struck it with one hand and his hand stuck to it. "Let me go. If you do not let me go I will strike you with my other hand," he said, and he struck it with that hand. When he hit it that hand also stuck. "Let me go. Stop holding me. If you do not let me go I will kick you," he said, and he kicked it. When he kicked it his foot stuck. "If you do not let go I will kick you with my other foot," he said, and he kicked it with that foot. When he did so his other foot stuck. "Let me go," he said, "I have my head left, and if you do not let me go I will butt you." He pulled back and forth to get free and butted it with his head and his head stuck. Then he hung there all doubled up.

While he was hanging there day came. And when it was light the water watchers came and found Rabbit hanging there. They picked him up, made a prisoner of him, and carried him off. They assembled together to kill him.

"Let us throw him into the fire," they said, but Rabbit laughed and replied, "Nothing can happen to me there. That is where I travel around."

"If that is the case we must kill him some other way," they said, and after they had debated a long time concluded, "Let us tie a rock around his neck and throw him into the water," but Rabbit laughed and called out, "I live all the time in water. Nothing can happen to me there." "Well," they said, "he will be hard to kill. How can we kill him?" After all had conferred for a while, they said, "I wonder what would become of him if we threw him into a brier patch?"

At that Rabbit cried out loudly. "Now you have killed me," he said.

"Now we have killed him," they replied. "If we had known that at first we would have had him killed already," so they carried him to a brier thicket, Rabbit weeping unceasingly as he was dragged along. Then they threw him into the brier thicket with all their strength, and he fell down, got up, and ran off at once, whooping.

Source: Adapted from "The Tar Baby," John R. Swanton. *Myths and Tales of the Southeastern Indians* (Washington, DC: Smithsonian Institution. Bureau of American Ethnology. Bulletin 88. U.S. Government Printing Office. 1929), pp. 104–105.

Red Feather

Contact between African Americans, European Americans, and Native Americans has led to an amalgamation of cultural traditions throughout the history of the United States. Runaway slaves were given refuge by Native Americans. Free Americans of African descent often shared common cause with Native Americans and gave them their support. Intermarriage between these two groups and European Americans fostered an exchange not only of DNA, but of folklore. The following tale was collected in nineteenth-century Missouri by Mary Owens from Madame Angelique Bougareau ("Big Angy"), a storyteller of African, Native American (Iowa), and "Missouri-French" descent. The tale is told in response to a conversation about "conjuration" (for further information, see "Possessed of Two Spirits"). The plot, however, is distributed widely among Native American Plains and Prairie cultures. Cross-culturally, heroes of mixed human and divine ancestry who bring gifts such as those Red Feather brought to his mother's people are labeled Culture Heroes.

Aunt Mymee said that she did not often eat wild cherries, that she had known of people who ate them falling at once into a deep sleep, especially if they were under the tree, and waking up to find that they had been "tricked" (conjured) by some unknown agency, and, of course, if you did not know how you were tricked, nor who did it, you never could get free.

"That so! That so!" exclaimed Big Angy, eagerly. "That what happen with Little Dove. Me mama told me that, long time back."

This is the story Big Angy told.

In the old time there was a young maiden called Little Dove. She was the most beautiful maiden in all the land and had many suitors, but she cared for none of them, and refused to go with them or accept their presents, or listen to their music. She was an only daughter. Her father loved her very much and would not urge her to marry. The other girls were displeased at this. They wished her to marry; for so long as she remained single the young men would look at no one else; they felt a great hatred and jealousy of her, but this they kept secret and were careful to praise her openly and seem to be her friends. They did not tell their real thoughts at all to the old people, though they had no scruples about admitting them to one another.

One day all the girls went out to gather the little black cherries. The birds had been before them and they found but few. They scattered into companies of small numbers to hunt more trees. Little Dove felt hurt that no one asked her to go along as a companion, and wandered off alone.

After a little search, she saw a fine tree growing at the edge of a very deep ravine cut into the soft soil by a feeble little stream. She set down her basket and tried to shake the glistening cherries from the branches. The tree was so strong and firmly rooted she could not shake it enough to bring down any fruit. She stood off and looked at it as she rested from her labors. Those cherries were the finest she had ever seen.

Alas! They were all growing well out of reach instead of some being on the drooping lower limbs. She felt that she must have them. Again and again she strove to shake the tree.

She could not. She flung sticks among the branches. Not one cherry fell. She thought she would go away and find another tree, but a great longing for the fruit of that particular one constrained her, and as often as her reluctant feet turned away they turned back again. She tried to climb the tree, but the trunk was as smooth as ice. She sat down and wept childish tears of disappointment and vexation.

So absorbed was she that she failed to observe that a young man in all the bravery of a warrior's apparel was coming up the steep, high bank of the little stream. He approached and called her by her name. She looked up in surprise. She did not know the stranger. She saw that he was handsome and very well dressed. His cheeks and the feathers in his scalp-lock were painted red. His leggings and shirt were whitened doeskin, his moccasins and blanket were embroidered with porcupine quills.

"Why do you weep?" he asked, and his voice was pleasant.

She hung her head, ashamed to answer, but at last his look compelled her. She told him her wish with regard to the cherries. At once he set his foot against the tree and the fruit fell about them in showers. She forgot the warrior, she forgot everything in her eagerness to possess that which she had craved; she gathered it hurriedly, she ate of it hungrily.

Then a rushing sound came in her ears. Frightened, she looked up from the ground where she sat and saw the warrior coming towards her with his arms outstretched. She fell forward. She knew no more.

When the new moon that shone the night before the cherry-picking was old, she went home to her father. She had been searched for. She had been mourned as dead. At first she was joyfully received, but when she affirmed she had been gone but a few hours, the faces of the old people grew grave, the young people became scornful. Her father withdrew into a dark corner, her brothers went away by themselves. She had no mother to reproach her else she might have heard bitter things. Then an old woman told her how

So the son stayed in the high habitation of the father, learning of peace and war and all that pertained to success in each. One thing only that the father knew he would not teach the son (whom he named "Redfeather"): he would not teach him how to assume the form of a bird. "Not yet, my son," he said. "Not until you come again."

When Redfeather seemed well enough instructed, his father conducted him as far as the treetop and there took leave of him. "Go to your mother's people," he said, at parting, "and instruct them as I have instructed you. Put them above their enemies, make them so that their young men shall, in future, know as much as the old ones do now, and that the old ones shall have wisdom beyond measurement. When this has been accomplished you may take your choice, either to stay with them or lead your mother up here." After saying this the father went back, and Redfeather descended the tree.

When he had finished relating all that had befallen him, Redfeather wished to set out immediately to find his people, who had moved a long way off, but his mother objected. She had not forgotten those last unhappy days she spent among them, therefore she did not wish to rejoin them nor have her son with them. When Redfeather found his arguments went for nought, he left her under the tree.

"Here you will find me on your return," she told him, for she had no faith in those people.

He set out buoyant of heart. He found the people. He taught them. He led them to battle. He helped them to conquer their enemies. He let them keep all the spoils of war. He showed them pleasant places in which to dwell. At first they were thankful. Then they were proud. Then they were jealous. Then they plotted against him.

He found out all these things. He called them together and revealed his knowledge of their plots. He renounced them. The wife he married he sent back to her father. He left all behind and returned to his mother. He found her sitting lonely under the elm tree, which was again black with cherries.

"Come up!" a voice called to her.

"I could not climb the tree when I was young, how can I now that I am old?" said Little Dove, weeping bitterly. "Go, my son, without me."

Redfeather took her hand. "Come up," he said, echoing the voice. He started, drawing her after him.

She found she could go easily; so they went, the son first, the mother after; up the trunk, the limbs, the light branches, through the thick leaves.

Some who had pursued Redfeather saw a cloud receive the two. With them went all the good luck of Little Dove's people.

Source: Adapted from *Old Rabbit the Voodoo and Other Sorcerers,* Mary A. Owen (New York: G. P. Putnam's Sons, 1893), pp. 44–50.

Clever Jack

As a trickster hero, Clever Jack shares common traits with Rabbit and the other animal tricksters of African American folklore. He uses his wits to overcome his superiors in the social hierarchy, and he is not troubled when, to do so, he ignores the conventional morality that binds the rest of the community. The set of adventures detailed in the following narrative, however, bear the marks of European rather than African influence.

Now there was a man, a very poor man, and his name was Jack. He thought of a scheme; he told his wife, "We are gonna try to get some money out of the king. We've got an old hog; we're gonna kill this hog and gonna catch the blood into the hog's bladder, you see, and I'm gonna place the bladder at your left side."

So he went along the street playing the fiddle, his wife going along with him. He played, "Middy-yum, yiddy-yum, yiddy-yum, yiddy-yum." So he drew the king's attention.

The king said, "Hello, m' boy."

Jack replied, "Hello, King."

King said, "What is your name?"

He replied, "Jack."

The king says, "You play the fiddle for a living?"

Jack says, "Yessir."

And the wife she says, "And I dance for a living." So he began to playing a tune, and his wife started to dancing.

So Jack told his wife, "Aw, you ain't dancing right." Him and his wife they get in a quarrel. He pulls up a big knife and stuck his wife in that bladder she had in her clothes. The wife fell out like she was dead and she starts bleeding.

The king says, "Oh, Jack, you done killed your wife, and you're in my land, and I'm compelled to prosecute you."

So Jack said, "Aw, I got a tune to bring her back." So he started playing his fiddle and dancing an singing, He sang,

"Ol' Bill done crossed the road,
Ol' Bill done crossed the road,
Ol' Bill done crossed the road."

So first his wife commenced moving her clothes; next she jumped up and started dancing. So she danced, danced, danced till she got tired.

So the king gets wild over the fiddle. He says, "Jack, want to sell that fiddle?"

Jack says, "Yes, for five thousand dollars."

So the king buys the fiddle and gives Jack five thousand dollars for it.

So Jack said, "I'll be dogged if that ain't one fool we got." So the king goes home and kills two of his servants. So he played, played, played, and his servants ain't never got back to life.

So he put out a big reward for Jack and had Jack caught. So after they caught Jack he cried and went on so pitiful that the king's two daughters begged him not to have Jack killed. So the king decided to let Jack live. He put him in the woods with the cattle and made him watch 'em. So Jack went out in the woods to watch the cattle.

Finally there was plenty water back there. There come up a big drought. All the cattle were dying. One of the king's daughters said, "Well, better let Jack carry the cattle out o' the woods to the water, that'll keep 'em from dying."

So Jack drove 'em out every day. So Jack had bought a poor cow named All Mine. He driven her in front of his cattle.

So he would call out every now and then, "Ho ho, All Mine! All Mine!"

And people came along and said, "Phew, but ain't that a rich man; just look at the cattle he's got."

Then Jack met another man and did the same trick with the hog bladder he had played on the king. This time he got one hundred thousand dollars. Later on when the man wanted to prosecute Jack, Jack said he didn't belong to himself, he belonged to the king. The fellow let him alone, because he didn't want trouble with the king.

Jack showed up one day with his pile of money in front of the king. The king was amazed and said, "Jack, where did you get all that money?"

Jack said, "I killed All Mine and sold her. I got so much for every pound o' meat and a cent for every hair on the cow." So the king jumps in and has about fifty cows killed. He couldn't sell the meat let alone the hairs. So the king concluded to get rid of Jack.

But once again one of his daughters stepped in. She said, "Put him in the garden. We can watch him there, and that will keep him out of devilment."

So they put him in the garden. Every day the women gave Jack a lot of orders like women will do. So one day Jack got mad and he said, "My God, you two are the most ugly things I ever did see. By God, you ought to stay out o' my sight, I'd like you much better." The two daughters were very pretty and felt highly insulted.

So they went to the king and said, "Father, we don't care what you do with Jack. You can take him and do what you want to."

So the king said, "Aha, I would certainly like to get rid of that fellow." So he concluded he would grab Jack and put him in a sack. After he caught Jack in a sack, he drove to about as deep a place as they was around the lake shore. He got out to get a drink at a cafe, and left Jack in the sack. Everybody around there knowed the king's daughter was real pretty. So a fellow was riding by on a horse.

Just as he rode by Jack cried out from the sack, "I don't want to marry the king's daughter, I don't want to marry the king's daughter, I don't want to marry the king's daughter."

When he heard Jack say that, the man stepped down from his horse and said, "What you say?"

Jack said, "I don't want to marry the king's daughter."

So the man said, "Well I would like to marry the king's daughter."

Jack said, "Well, untie me real quick, and you can take my place in the sack. The king's inside the cafe." The man untied the sack and Jack came out and the man went in. Jack lit on the horse and rode away real quick. The king came out and had Jack dropped in the deepest place in the lake. He said, "Well, I'm through with you. I done seen the last bubble. I'll not be bothered with you any more." He left the river and went on his way.

Jack had plenty money, so he went away. Six months later he came back. He had a big drove of sheep. Jack wouldn't go into the king's place, but he stayed out on the highway, and he sent someone in and asked him if he wanted to buy some sheep. The king was surprised to see Jack alive again.

He said, "Jack, I thought I drowned you six months ago." Jack said, "You did. And where you throwed me they was all kind of animals. The sheep was the easiest to drive so I brought them to you. I thought you might want to buy some sheep."

The king said, "Jack, I'm gonna buy these sheep from you, but I don't ever want to catch your feet on my land any more."

So Jack goes to Europe after this, and there he bought a carriage to ride in just like the king's. On the bottom of the carriage he plastered some land that he took from Europe. Then, Jack drove back to the king's land and called the king.

The king said, "I wonder if this is Jack again." Sure enough it was Jack. The king said, "Jack, didn't I tell you that I didn't ever want to catch your feet on my land any more."

Jack said, "Pardon me, my feet are not on your land, I brought my land with me."

Then the king let Jack alone. He gave him up.

Source: Adapted from "Little Claus," Arthur Huff Fauset. "Negro Folk Tales from the South (Alabama, Mississippi, Louisiana)," *Journal of American Folklore* 40 (1927): 213–303, pp. 253–255.

Jean Sotte

In both African and European descended communities of Louisiana, Jean Sotte (Louisiana French Creole, "Foolish John") commonly plays the role of numskull. In some cases, however, the foolishness is merely a disguise for guile. Like the other tricksters mentioned in the following tale (Lapin, Bouki, and Renard), Jean Sotte is a "wise fool" who turns others' preconceptions of his inferiority into a strategy for success. This strategy may well have struck a familiar chord for the African American community.

There was once a fellow who was so foolish that everybody called him Jean Sotte. He was so simple that every one made fun of him. He would light the lamp in daytime, and put it out at night; he would take an umbrella with him only when it was very dark. In summer he would put on a great coat, and in winter he would go around nearly naked. In short, he did everything contrary to common sense. King Bangon, who loved to play tricks, heard of the sayings and deeds of Jean Sotte, and sent for him to amuse his friends. When Jean came to the king all began to laugh, as he looked so awkward. The king asked him if he knew how to count. Jean replied that he knew how to count eggs; that yesterday he had found four and two.

"How much does that make?" said the king.

Jean went to count the eggs, and on returning said there were four and two.

"Exactly," said the king, "but tell me, Jean Sotte, they say that Compair Lapin (Brother Rabbit) is your father?"

"Yes, he is."

"No, no," said someone else; "I think it is Compair Bouki (Hyena)."

"Yes, yes," said Jean Sotte; "it is he also."

"No, no," said an old woman who was passing; "it is Renard (Fox) who is your father."

"Yes," said Jean Sotte, "all of them; they are all my fathers. Every time one of them passes by me he says, 'Good-morning, my child.' I must believe, then, that they are all my fathers."

Everybody laughed at Jean Sotte; then the king said: "Jean Sotte, I want you to bring me tomorrow morning a bottle of bull's milk. It is to make a drug for my daughter, who is sick, and has a sideache in her back."

"All right," said Jean Sotte, "tomorrow morning early I shall bring it."

King Bangon then said "On the first of April, in one month, you will come. I want you to guess something. If you guess, I will give you my daughter in marriage, but if you try three times, and do not succeed, my executioner will have to cut your neck."

"All right," said Jean Sotte, "I will try." And then he went away, pretending to go and get the bull's milk.

When he reached home, he related to his mother all that had happened, and the old woman began to cry, and could not be consoled, because, however foolish her boy was, she loved him, as he was her only child. She forbade him to go to the king, and threatened to tie him in her cabin, or to have the sheriff throw him in prison. Jean Sotte paid no attention to his mother, and started before day break, with his axe on his shoulder. He soon arrived at the house of the king, and he climbed into a big oak-tree which was before the door. He began to cut down the branches with his axe, and he woke up everybody in the house.

One of the servants of the king came out to see what was the matter; and when he saw Jean Sotte on the top of the tree, he said, "But what is your business there? Fool that you are, you are disturbing everybody."

"It is not your business. Do you hear?" said Jean Sotte. "Are you the watchdog to be barking thus in the yard? When your master, King Bangon, comes, I will tell him what I am doing here."

The king came out, and asked Jean Sotte what he was doing there. He replied that he was cutting the bark to make some tea for his father, who had been delivered the day before of two twins.

"What!" said the king, "for whom do you take me, Jean Sotte. Where did you ever hear of a man in childbirth? I think you mean to make fun of me."

"How is it that yesterday you asked a bottle of bull's milk? If you were right, I am also."

The king replied, "I believe that you are not so foolish as you want to make people believe. Go to the kitchen, and they will give you your breakfast. Don't forget to come on the first of April, that we may see which of us will be the April fool."

On the first of April Jean Sotte mounted his horse and went out without his mother seeing him. Compair Bouki, who is deceitful and evil-minded, said, "I shall prevent Jean Sotte from going, because I know he is so foolish that they will cut his neck and keep his horse. It is better that I should profit by it, and take his horse. Don't you say anything; you will see what I shall do.

He took a large basket full of poisoned cakes, and put it on a bridge where Jean Sotte was to pass. "If he eats those cakes he will die, and I shall take the horse." Bouki knew that Jean Sotte was greedy and that he would surely eat the cakes.

Compair Lapin liked Jean Sotte, because one day when he was caught in a snare Jean Sotte freed him. He did not forget that, and said: "I want to protect the poor fellow, "and before daybreak he waited on the road for Jean Sotte. When he saw him, he said: "Jean Sotte, I am coming to render you a service, listen to me. Don't eat or drink anything on your way, even if you are dying of hunger and of thirst; and when the king will ask you to guess, you will reply what I am going to tell you. Come near; I don't want anybody to hear."

Compair Lapin then told him what to say. "Yes, yes, I understand," said Jean Sotte, and he began to laugh.

"Now," said Compair Lapin, "don't forget me when you marry the king's daughter; we can have good business together."

"Yes," said Jean Sotte, "I shall not forget you."

"Well, good luck, pay attention to all you see, look on all sides, and listen well."

Then Jean Sotte started, and a little while afterwards he arrived at a bridge on the river. The first thing he saw was the basket full of cakes which Compair Bouki had placed there. They smelled good and they were very tempting. Jean Sotte touched them and felt like biting one, but he remembered what Compair Lapin had told him. He stopped a moment and said, "Let me see if they will do harm to my horse." He took half a dozen cakes and gave them to his horse. The poor beast died almost immediately and fell on the bridge. "See, if I had not been prudent, it is I who would be dead instead of my horse. Ah! Compair Lapin was right; a little more and I should have been lost. Now I shall have to go on foot."

Before he started he threw his horse into the river, and as the poor beast was being carried away by the current, three buzzards alighted on the horse and began to eat him. Jean Sotte looked at him a long time, until he disappeared behind the point in the river. "Compair Lapin told me, 'listen, look, and don't say anything;' all right, I shall have something to ask the king to guess."

When Jean Sotte came to the king nobody was trying to guess, for all those who had tried three times had been put to death by the king's executioner. Fifty men already had been killed, and everyone said, on seeing Jean Sotte, "There is Jean Sotte who is going to try, they will surely cut off his head, for he is so foolish. But so much the worse for him if he is such a fool."

When he saw Jean Sotte the king began to laugh and told him to come nearer. "What is it," said he, "that early in the morning walks on four legs, at noon on two, and in the evening on three legs?"

If I guess, you will give me your daughter?"

"Yes," said the king.

"Oh! That is nothing to guess."

"Well, hurrah! Hurry on if you don't want me to cut your neck."

Jean Sotte told him, it was a child who walked on four legs; when he grew up he walked on two, and when he grew old he had to take a stick, and that made three legs.

All remained with their mouths wide open, they were so astonished.

"You have guessed right; my daughter is for you. Now, let anybody ask me something, as I know everything in the world; if I do not guess right 1 will give him my kingdom and my fortune."

Jean Sotte said to the king, "I saw a dead being that was carrying three living beings and was nourishing them. The dead did not touch the land and was not in the sky; tell me what it is, or I shall take your kingdom and your fortune."

King Bangon tried to guess; he said this and that and a thousand things, but he had to give it up. Jean Sotte said then, "My horse died on a bridge, I threw him into the river, and three buzzards alighted on him and were eating him up in the river. They did not touch the land and they were not in the sky."

Everybody saw that Jean Sotte was smarter than all of them together. He married the king's daughter, took his place, and governed the kingdom. He took Compair Lapin as his first overseer, and hanged Compair Bouki for his rascality. After that they changed Jean Sotte's name and called him Jean l'Esprit.

Source: Adapted from "Jean Sotte," Alcée Fortier. *Louisiana Folk-Tales* (Boston & New York, American Folk-Lore Society, 1895), pp 63–69.

Jackskin

The tale of "Jackskin" is known in European tradition as "Catskin." The plot of the heroine abused by the unnatural behavior of a relative and saved by a magical benefactor closely resembles the more well-known "Cinderella." When "Jackskin" was orally transmitted from European American to African American communities, the medieval setting of the tale was adapted to the rural surroundings of the African American performer from whom the story was collected in the early twentieth century.

There was a man had a daughter and a wife. His wife died. The daughter was the picture of his wife. So his wife said, "If you marry again I don't want you to marry anyone but someone who resembles me." So he roamed the world through but he couldn't find no one but his daughter who looked like his wife.

So he went to his daughter finally and said, "I want to get married, but your mother said I should not marry anybody who didn't look like her; so I'm compelled to marry you."

She went to her godmother and said, "Oh, godmother, what shall I do? My father wants to marry me."

Her godmother said, "You tell him you will marry him, but he must get you a speaking looking glass." So she went back to her father and told him. He found a speaking looking glass and came to marry her.

She went back to her godmother and said, "Oh, godmother, what shall I do? My father wants to marry me."

Her godmother said, "He must kill this jack [donkey], take the hide, and have you a dress made out of it."

So the father had the jack killed, and he took its hide and made a dress out of it for his daughter. Oh, she went all to pieces.

She went and told her godmother and her godmother said, "Now you tell him to find you a ring that will fit the finest bird that flies in the air."

The father went out and searched until he found the ring.

The girl got really disgusted by now, and she went and told her godmother. Her godmother said, "Now I tell you what you do. You appoint the wedding day, the day that you gonna get married. Now his room is upstairs, so you dress downstairs and let the looking glass be down stairs."

On the wedding day the girl locked the room up and put the looking glass in it; let on she was in there dressing.

Pretty soon the father called down, "Are you ready yet?"

The looking glass said, "Not quite." Every time he called again the looking glass would say, "Not quite." About five hours passed that he thought she was dressing.

Finally the father got mad and he broke down the door and rushed in the room. He discovered how he had been tricked and he smashed the glass and started after her.

When she ran away she came to a king's palace. She had a beautiful face, but then she had a jack skin suit on. She walked up and asked the king's wife to give her a job. At that time the king's son, he was a sport—walked in. All the rest of the people was looking at her clothes, but he looked at her beautiful face. The king's wife said to her, "We have no job to give you."

Then the prince said, "We need a boy in the turkey house in the back woods." (The prince was a hunter). So the mother accepted. She told one of the help to go back there and show Jackskin where the house was.

Every day the prince had a habit of hunting. He went back there to the turkey house. And when the girl went to her room he looked through the keyhole, and lo! She shook and different dresses the color of fair weather came to replace the jack skin clothes, and she looked like a beautiful girl once more.

After this, the prince went home and he was taken sick. They sent for a doctor. Doctor said, "Nothing wrong with him, it's only that he's in love with someone."

So his mother said, "Who in the name of God is he in love with?" He had to hide that he was in love with Jackskin so it made him sick. He didn't say anything. In about two or three days he said he felt like eating a cake. He had a craving for some girl's cake, he didn't know what girl. His parents sent and got all the popular girls and had them make cake. None of the cakes suited him.

He said "But you haven't sent for Jackskin."

They said, "What you want with that stinking girl around the house?" But they went sure enough and got Jackskin. They got her, in her Jackskin suit, and she made a cake and dropped her ring in there. So that was the first cake he would eat a piece of. Biting that piece of cake he bit on the ring. He took it and kissed it and slipped it under the pillow of his sickbed.

Then later he showed the ring up. He said he had eaten the cake, and the ring was in it. He said the finger the ring would fit that's the girl he wanted for his wife. So they called for all the girls to come to the palace. All the girls they came, and they all tried to get that ring on their fingers, all with the exception of Jackskin. None of them could get the ring on.

Then the prince said, "Where is Jackskin ? Send for her."

Everybody said, "Aw you want her! You ought to be ashamed of yourself."

The prince asked until they called for her. When she came she had on little slippers She slipped the ring on her fingers, then shook herself, and they couldn't look at her. They had to turn their faces she was glittering so. Then she had that beautiful face and dresses that shined like the sun. So she married the prince and they all lived happily ever after.

Source: Adapted from "Little Claus," Arthur Huff Fauset. "Negro Folk Tales from the South (Alabama, Mississippi, Louisiana)," *Journal of American Folklore* 40 (1927): 213–303, pp. 244–245.

The Elephant and the Whale

"The Elephant and the Whale" is distributed throughout the American South, the West Indies, and African South America. The trickster, in this case Compair Lapin (the creole Brother Rabbit) indulges in a favorite pastime of stirring up trouble by issuing false challenges that pit unwitting competitors against each other. Along the way, there is another object lesson concerning the power of brain over brawn. Compair Lapin's companion, toady, and frequent victim is Bouki (Wolof, "Hyena"). The incorporation of this folktale character and the Wolof word for him demonstrates the enduring influence of West African traditional culture on this body of African American folklore.

One day Compair Lapin and Compair Bouki were going on a journey together. Compair Lapin often took Bouki with him to make fun of him, and to hear all the news which Bouki knew. When they reached the seashore, they saw something which was very strange, and which astonished them so much that they stopped to watch and listen. It was an elephant and a whale which were conversing together.

"You see," said Bouki, "they are the two largest beasts in the world, and the strongest of all animals."

"Hush up," said Lapin, "let us go nearer and listen. I want to hear what they are saying."

The elephant said to the whale: "Commère Baleine (Louisiana French Creole, "Sister Whale"), as you are the largest and strongest in the sea, and I am the largest and strongest on land, we must rule over all beasts; and all those who will revolt against us we shall kill them, you hear, commère."

"Yes, Compair; keep the land and I shall keep the sea."

"You hear," said Bouki, "let us go, because it will be bad for us if they hear that we are listening to their conversation."

"Oh! I don't care," said Lapin. "I am more cunning than they; you will see how I am going to fix them."

"No," said Bouki, "I am afraid, I must go."

"Well, go, if you are so good for nothing and cowardly; go quickly, I am tired of you; you are too foolish."

Compair Lapin went to get a very long and strong rope, then he got his drum and hid it in the grass. He took one end of the rope and went to the elephant: "Mister Elephant, you who are so good and so strong. I wish you would render me a service; you would relieve me of a great trouble and prevent me from losing my money."

The elephant was glad to hear such a fine compliment, and he said: "Compair, I shall do for you everything you want. I am always ready to help my friends."

"Well," said Lapin, "I have a cow which is stuck in the mud on the coast; you know that I am not strong enough to pull her out; I come for you to help me. Take this rope in your trunk. I shall tie it to the cow, and when you hear me beat the drum, pull hard on the rope. I tell you that because the cow is stuck deep in the mud."

"That is all right," said the elephant. "I shall pull the cow out, or the rope will break."

Compair Lapin took the other end of the rope and ran towards the sea. He paid a pretty compliment to the whale, and asked her to render him the same service about the cow, which was stuck in a bayou in the woods. Compair Lapin's mouth was so honeyed that no one could refuse him anything. The whale took hold of the rope and said, "When I shall hear the drum beat I shall pull."

"Yes," said Lapin, "begin pulling gently, and then more and more."

"You need not be afraid," said the whale; "I shall pull out the cow, even if the Devil were holding her."

"That is good," said Lapin; "we are going to laugh." And he beat his drum.

The elephant began to pull so hard that the rope was like a bar of iron. The whale, on her side, was pulling and pulling, and yet she was coming nearer to the land, as she was not so well situated to pull as the elephant. When she saw that she was mounting on land, she beat her tail furiously and plunged headlong into the sea. The shock was so great that the elephant was dragged to the sea.

"What," said he, "what is the matter? That cow must be wonderfully strong to drag me so. Let me kneel with my front feet in the mud."

Then he twisted the rope round his trunk in such a manner that he pulled the whale again to the shore. He was very much astonished to see his friend the whale. "What is the matter," said he. "I thought it was Compair Lapin's cow I was pulling."

"Lapin told me the same thing. I believe he is making fun of us."

"He must pay for that," said the elephant. "I forbid him to eat a blade of grass on land because he laughed at us."

"And I will not allow him to drink a drop of water in the sea. We must watch for him, and the first one that sees him must not miss him."

Compair Lapin said to Bouki, "It is growing hot for us; it is time to leave."

"You see," said Bouki, "you are always bringing us into trouble."

"Oh, hush up! I am not through with them yet; you will see how I shall fix them."

They went on their way and after a while they separated. When Compair Lapin arrived in the wood, he found a little dead deer. The dogs had bitten him so that the hair had fallen off his skin in many places. Lapin took off the deer's skin and put it on his back. He looked exactly like a wounded deer. He passed limping by the elephant, who said to him, "Poor little deer, how sick you look."

"Oh yes! I am suffering very much; you see it is Compair Lapin who poisoned me and put his curse on me, because I wanted to prevent him from eating grass, as you had ordered me. Take care, Mr. Elephant, Compair Lapin has made a bargain with the Devil; he will be hard on you, if you don't take care."

The elephant was very much frightened. He said, "Little deer, you will tell Compair Lapin that I am his best friend; let him eat as much grass as he wants and present my compliments to him"

The deer met a little later the whale in the sea. "But poor little deer, why are you limping so; you seem to be very sick."

"Oh, yes! It is Compair Lapin who did that. Take care, Commere Baleine."

The whale also was frightened, and said, "I want to have nothing to do with the Devil; please tell Compair Lapin to drink as much water as he wants."

The deer went on his way, and when he met Compair Bouki he took off the deer's skin and said: "You see that I am more cunning than all of them, and that I can make fun of them all the time. Where I shall pass another will be caught."

"You are right indeed," said Compair Bouki.

Source: Adapted from "The Elephant and the Whale," Alcée Fortier. *Louisiana Folk-Tales* (Boston & New York, American Folk-Lore Society, 1895), pp. 3–7.

John the Fool and John the Smart

As the result of historical events (the American and Haitian Wars for independence in the late eighteenth century, for example) and continuing trade, Creole culture in the American South was influenced by folktales from the French Caribbean. One such case, "John the Fool and John the Smart," reveals a relationship comparable to that between Compair Lapin and Bouki. The Haitian characters of Ti- Malice, the clever trickster, and Bouki (spelled Buki in ths tale), the genuine fool, influenced the development of the Lapin and Bouki in Louisiana Creole narratives (see, for example, "Compair Lapin and the Earthworm" and "The Elephant and the Whale"). Echoes of John the Fool, moreover, are apparent in "Jean Sotte."

Voila! There was a very old woman who had twin boys, one was called John the Fool, the other John the Smart. John the Fool used to stay at home with his mother to watch the shop, John the Smart used to go to the market.

One day John the Smart was sick, he sent his brother. John the Fool asked for a lot of money for all the purchases he thought necessary. His mother gave him a large quantity of two-cob coins, amounting to three gourdins. He set forth.

"Thus, if I meet some beggars, I shall have enough money to give them." This idea in his head, before turning the crossroad he thought he had heard one. He did not turn back but looked aside and saw his shadow walking behind him.

"Very well, you may go, here are two cobs!"

He threw away two cobs and walked on. At another crossroad he again saw his shadow.

"I am in a hurry, dear, I cannot stay. Here are two cobs, take it all the same!" He threw away the money and went on. Each time he had this thought he looked aside and saw his shadow.

"What a lot of beggars! It is a procession! Why do these people walk like that behind me? Maybe my brother told them I had some money."

When he had only two gourdins more, he told the shadow:

"Friend, I have already given away all my money, go to my home to get some more."

The shadow still followed him.

"How stubborn this man is!"

John the Fool turned round angrily, the shadow disappeared. "When a man knows how to speak with people. I am a superman!"

When he reached the market he thought his brother had asked for spinach. They sold him a small bundle for ten cobs. He chided : "Thieves! You have me pay ten cobs for a tiny bundle of weeds. I do not want it. Keep your thing!"

He entered a small shop where they sold tafia. He asked some for ten cobs. They poured it in his bottle. The liquid reached the height of two spread fingers. The man was dissatisfied.

"How stupid I would be to stay here and lose my money! Madam, I am not asking for alms, I am buying, take back your thing and return my money."

The merchant protested shouting, John the Fool shouted back. He had the woman take back her tafia to get his bottle. Disgusted he went away. On the roadside he saw wild spinach, he plucked it and filled his bottle in the river.

When he reached home John the Smart asked: "Where are the goods I asked you to buy?"

"These people are thieves. They thought they could deceive me. They sold for spinach a handful of weeds and wanted me to pay quite a sum' for it. If you want weeds, here are some, gratis! They gave me two fingers of tafia for ten cobs, I left it to them, here is God's tafia gratis! I had forgotten the other errands..."

"Where is my money?"

"Your money? As soon as I had passed the door a lot of beggars set to walk behind me, I gave them the whole money. There is two gourdins left, take them!"

"John the Fool, my poor brother! I am obliged to go to town, you will stay here to give mother her bath. Don't forget, a lukewarm bath!"

Now the old lady was paralyzed, she could watch the shop but one had to help her to get dressed, to eat, to walk, she could not even blow her nose alone. John the Fool put water on the fire, he had his mother sit at the bottom of the bath and threw a boilerful of hot water upon her. The old lady died without a word.

"How pleased mother is with her bath! Look at her laugh, she cannot close her mouth. Let me give you your pipe!"

He did not wait for an answer and thrust the old woman's pipe down into her throat.

"When you want to get out, call me to help you!"

He sat down at the door sill and forgot the mother. When John the Smart came back he told him: "My dear! How happy the old lady is about her bath! She laughed so much that her mouth remained opened. I gave her pipe."

John the Smart, who knew his brother, felt uncomfortable and ran into the house.

"Mother, Mother!" He came nearer: "John the Fool, the old woman is dead, you have killed our mother!" John the Fool burst into shrieks (if I may say so without lacking respect for the audience).

"Don't cry, poor brother, it is not your fault, God has made you this way, I ought not to forget that."

They made the funeral and sold the house to get some money: John the Smart wanted to travel. He gathered all his clothes in a big bundle and put all his money in a silk handkerchief which he placed in the middle of the bundle. John the Fool took his game cock, his razor and a calabash of water. While walking John the Smart said: "I have forgotten my pot!"

Now if you are looking for an obliging man and do not take John the Fool you will not find any. He darted homeward and came back with a door on his back.

"What do you want me to do with that?"

"Did you not ask for your door?"

"How foolish! Take the door back where it belongs, it will hinder our walking."

"No! I will not make this journey another time!"

They walked a great deal. Night came. They saw a big wood and as they were afraid of beasts and of bad people they climbed up a tree. This tree was a very large kapok tree; they sat in a fork, John the Fool pulled up the door and held it upright in the branches. He put the cock in the pocket of his jacket and the calabash in the pocket of his trousers. They slept.

In the middle of the night they heard some noise and got up. (Under the tree) they saw a big trestle table with cloth, silver-plate and all kinds of good things to eat or drink. In a corner there were four big bags well tied up. A great quantity of small devils were frolicking around the table. How they were frolicking!

John the Smart said: "I want some wine! I am thirsty for wine."

"I do not have any, here is water!"

John the Fool passed the calabash. He took it awkwardly, the water fell on the tablecloth of the devils. They laughed merrily. "Here is the dew! Our business is blessed!"

All of them got up, they began to dance and to sing and made a large ring around the table. John the Fool wanted to see everything but the table prevented it.

"I will let it fall!"

"Look out! Watch out for your life, these people will strangle you."

"Have you forgotten my razor?"

He dropped the door! It fell in the middle of the table, put out the lamp of the devils and crashed the glassware and china.

"Earthquake, earthquake!" The devils vanished away. John the Fool came down with his brother and they lighted a candle. John the Smart examined the bags, found them filled with money and put one into his bundle. John the Fool sat beside the table and ate till full. While he was eating, one of the devils came back. These devils were big-headed dwarfs of the size of a ten-year-old child with a long beard. The dwarf gazed for a long time. John the Fool shaved his beard with his razor. The devil laughed. John the Fool shaved half his beard and asked him:

"Do you want to shave? At your service. But before that I want to know only one thing, let me see the string of your tongue, open your mouth!"

The devil opened his mouth. John the Fool severed his tongue. The devil howled and ran to his people.

"What is the matter? Where is our money?"

"Tru-ru-ru-ru-ru!"

He showed them his maimed tongue. They sent another devil. Now John the Fool was eating in the dark with his brother, the lamp had remained on the table; when the devil arrived they saw him while he could not see them, they jumped on him and severed his tongue. John the Smart said: "Let us take all the bags and go away!"

"They are too heavy. My dear! I don't want to get sick!" They left.

They walked and walked. They reached a town where they did not see anybody. All the houses and shops were brightly lighted, there were lamps and candles everywhere but no man or animal was in sight.

As they stared at this, a calabash rolled near them. John the Fool touched his brother: "Take care of your feet!" Another calabash came to meet the first, there was a conversation. The brothers stayed on the side of the hilly road. Calabashes appeared tumbling down the slope, they came into collision, they gathered and whispered. The brothers did not understand a word.

Then a calabash marched up to John the Fool: "You are foreigners?"

"Yes, Mrs. Calabash. But, tell me, is there anything else than calabashes? I did not see anybody. How can a calabash speak?"

"Shut up, child! We are men like you but we are obliged to live in calabashes, the master of the town is a frightful devil. For six months we have been in the night, because fearing robbers he has hidden the key of daylight in the middle of his heart. If he were to find you here walking like a man surely he would eat you! Here are two empty calabashes, get in!"

John the Smart was a man who did not like to get into trouble. He asked, "How can we manage? We are too big."

"Look at this hole! Put the point of your foot into it, the whole foot will pass, push a little, the whole leg will pass, your body will reduce, it will grow smaller and smaller, push on, it will slip to the bottom of the calabash."

Smart did as he was told, these people were right, he disappeared into the hole. The Fool stood alone.

"Get into your house!"

"I, never! I am not a coward, the devil may kill me. I will not creep into a calabash. You are all dastards! All the men I have seen in the town let only one devil rule them this way? You consent to lose the daylight and live like beasts, what did I say? Worse than beasts, there are walking beasts, as for you, you can only roll. No, gentlemen, I will stay upright, if I die I will die like a man, not like a beast!"

At this moment, John the Fool's cock crowed: "Ko-kee-yoo-koo! Ko-kee-yoo-koo!"

The devil had given orders to kill all cocks, the crowd vanished. "This man is crazy! If the Master believes we are his accomplices he will kill us!"

The cock felt it was four o'clock, as he did not see the sun, he crowed again: "Ko-kee-yoo-koo!"

From very far a confused roar was heard in answer:

> I have told the day it would break no more
> I have told the day it would break no more
> Either on this side or on the other
> I have told the day it would break no more!

"Aha!" John the Fool also sang:

> I tell the day it must break anew
> I tell the day it must break anew
> Either on this side or on the other
> I tell the day it must break anew!

The devil's song was coming nearer and nearer, and always louder.

> I have told the day it would break no more
> I have told the day it would break no more
> Either on this side or on the other
> I have told the day it would break no more!

John the Fool swelled his whole body, he shouted so as to cover the voice of the devil.

> I tell the day it must break anew.
> I tell the day it must break anew
> Either on this side or on the other
> I tell the day it must break anew!

The devil appeared: he was taller than this house, when he sang everything shook.

> I have told the day it would break no more
> I have told the day it would break no more

Either on this side or on the other
I have told the day it would break no more!

John the Fool prepared his razor.

I tell the day it must break anew
I tell the day it must break anew
Either on this side or on the other
I tell the day it must break anew!

They fought relentlessly. John the Fool goaded him with his razor, he cut him, he carved him, he did not leave to the devil time enough to breathe. The devil was tired. The Fool plunged the razor into his temple, the Devil cried and died. The Fool hurled him on the ground and opened his heart, he found a small box with a tiny lock in which the key was hung. He turned the key and the sun shone, it was daylight.

During the time all these things were happening, John the Smart was talking merrily with the people (in the calabashes). They told him there was a king who ruled the country (before) the Devil came and stole the key of daylight. The king was greatly offended, but he was afraid to fight the devil, so he promised that the man who would bring back the key would marry his legitimate daughter. John the Smart approached his brother.

"Hand me the key, I want to see something!"

"Here it is!"

John the Fool did not look at him, he was lecturing the crowd. "Gentlemen, come out of your calabashes, don't be afraid, you are men anew. I am your chief, my brother is your lieutenant. Where has he gone? John the Smart, John the Smart!"

The Smart was far away. With his money he had hired a horse and rushed to the Palace. The guards stopped him.

"Tell the king I have come to him with news of his key."

The king came.

"What do you know?"

He held his tongue and handed the key.

"Where is the box?"

"Good Lord! I was galloping so fast that the box has dropped."

"Don't take it so to heart, that's nothing. I will have another one made, only the key was indispensable. Now tell me how you managed to kill this big devil."

John the Smart sat down. Everything the Fool had done he said it was himself. The King was glad, he called his children and his wife, introduced Monsieur and betrothed him to the girl.

John the Fool was looking for his brother. He left his money, his commanding position to walk and search. He stopped everybody he met to ask if they had not seen the other one.

"John the Smart is like Ti-Malice, he cannot be dead. I must find him!"

One day he was overtired, he sat down in a crossroad to eat a cassava soaked in cane syrup. He heard two women talking: "My dear, what a beautiful wedding it will be! These people have prepared such a quantity of food!"

John the Fool listened more carefully, his mouth watered. He understood it was the King's daughter who was to marry the man who had killed the devil, the same man who had caused the day to break. He felt unable to realize how this could be done: "I am the man they are talking about! I don't want to be married to somebody I do not know, to a girl I have never seen, she may be hunch-backed! I don't want, I do not want that at all! I am going to the King!"

He reached the Palace. The guards stopped him. "No trespassing. What do you want?"

"I want to speak to the King."

"Have you an appointment ? What have you to tell him?"

"Is that your business? What insolence! You don't want me to come in, very well I will call the King from here."

The fellow began to shout: "King, King! They oppose my entering here, come out to meet me! King, King!"

The soldiers tried to silence him, the more they tried, the more he shouted. The King appeared at the window.

"Let him speak. You, what do you want?"

"King, I heard everybody announce the wedding of your daughter with the man who had killed the devil who kept day from breaking. King, I am this man and I have come to tell you not to be in such a hurry. How could I want your daughter, I don't know her!"

"This man is mad!"

"You are the mad man! Listen, King, here is your box!"

"How did you lose the key?"

"It was never lost, I lent it to my brother who wanted to see how it was made."

John the Fool did not look like a liar. The King understood there was some deceit in the whole thing. He sent for his future son-in-law who came in splendidly dressed. John the Fool rushed to his neck: "Where were you! I thought you were lost. What fine clothes, dear, how elegant!"

"When will you stop with your bad manners? You have crumpled my jacket so it looks chawed by an ox."

The King asked them very severely: "Now, gentlemen, explain to me what I see. You wanted to fool me!"

John the Smart was ashamed but the Fool told the old man: "Is it your business, King? You have your key and you have your box. You had promised your daughter to the man who would bring back the key, he did it, give him your daughter, I will not be jealous!"

The Fool came a little nearer: "You had never spoken of the box, I have brought your box, you cannot leave me without compensation, do you have something for me?" "Listen! Both of you are twins, is it not true? You look so much alike. I will appoint you general, I have other daughters..."

"Ach, King! Ambition kills the rat. When I passed through the yard I smelt all kinds of good flavors, my heart was thrilled. Would you care to appoint me your kitchen inspector?"

"Oh! my...Buki is Buki."

Source: Adapted from "John the Fool and John the Smart," Suzanne Comhaire-Sylvain. "Creole Tales from Haiti," *Journal of American Folklore* 50 (1937): 207–295, pp. 274–281.

The Champion

*Comic narratives set in the plantation period and focused on the inter-
actions of Old Master and a clever slave were a popular tale type
among African Americans in the southern states. In many cases slave
and master were adversaries. In this instance, however, Bill and Old
Master work together in executing a plan developed by the bondsman
to overcome brawn with wit.*

The way it was, Old Master went out and bought him five hundred slaves
on this place. And the other captain over here bought him five hundred
slaves. And buying the five hundred slaves, this master has a big slave in
there he said was stouter than any slave that he had ever bought, and he's
the champion of that bunch. This master right across the fence on the next
plantation told him he had one there, listen, was stouter than the one the
first Master had there.

"Well," he says, "this one I got will whip that one you got."

"Well," the first master says, "I'll bet you one thousand dollars that mine,
listen, will whip that one you got, or else take his nerve so he won't fight."
Said, "I'll bet you, understand, this hand of mine will fight this one of yours
and whip him, or else I'll bet you five hundred dollars that when your hand
gets there he won't fight mine."

Other one says, "When we going to meet?'

Says, "Well, Friday, let's meet 'em and let 'em fight." Say, "You have all
your people on the place to meet 'em to fight, and I'm goin' to have all of
mine to see to fight, and me and you are goin' to be there."

Just before that Friday, next day, this first master's slave said. I don't
believe I can whip this other champion over yonder, but I can fix it so you'll
win the five hundred dollars if not the thousand. Just let me know where we
goin' to fight at." He said, "Give me your shovel and give me your ax."

He went down in the woods and dug up a water oak, a common tree in
those parts. He took a mule and drug it to a hole up there, and set it out in
the hole. And when he set it in the ground he put some leaves around to
make it look like the tree growed there. It wasn't goin' to wilt because it
wasn't more than twenty-four hours before they were going to fight. That

tree looked alive. Then he taken all his wife's white clothes and put them around there and set out a wash tub.

The next day when the master from the other plantation came for the fight, the first master came with his champion with a grass line tied on him. There was a little place in the grass line where it was weak. The master walked his champion up to the tree and tied him to it. The other champion from the next plantation was walkin' loose.

His master asked to the first one, "Is this the one goin' to fight my champion?"

Said, "Yeah."

Said, "Why you got him tied up that way?"

Said, "I'm scared he'll get frustrated and mad. He's ambitious and wants to fight. I'm scared he'll get loose and jump on your champion and hurt him. He's so stout I have to tie him so I can talk to him."

This other champion that come from the other plantation, he tell his master, "Death ain't but death. I ain't goin' to fight no man they got to tie to a tree, else he'll kill me, so you might just as well shoot me down where I am."

The first master say, "You want to see how stout my champion is before they fight?"

Other one say, "Yeah."

He say, "Well then, I'll make him try out that rope a little." Says to his champion, "Bill, pull against that tree a little so's this other champion can see what you are."

Bill braced his feet and pulled, and the tree start to lean. All them slaves from the other plantation backed up when they see that. Bill pulled some more, and the roots start to pop out of the ground.

The other champion got behind his master. Says, "Shoot me down, Master, cause that man goin' to kill me anyway. I ain't goin' to fight no man that pulls trees down by the roots."

His master say to the other one, "Your champion's scared mine 'bout to death. Don't let him pull no more."

But Bill gave another tug and that tree started to come down, and the rope broke at the thin place. He came runnin' at where the masters were standing.

The other master said, "And now I'm gettin' scared too. Hold him off. My champion ain't goin' to fight, so here's the five hundred dollars."

The first master tell all his hands to take Bill and hold him, and whilst they were doin' that the slaves from the other plantation just lit out for home. Bill didn't think he could whip the other champion, but he worked it out so the other one was scared to fight him, and that's how his master won five hundred dollars in the bet.

Source: Adapted from "The Champion," Harold Courlander. *A Treasury of Afro-American Folklore* (New York: Marlowe and Company, 1996 [1976]), pp. 434–435.

The Marriage of Compair Lapin

"The Marriage of Compair Lapin" combines features of African and European traditional narrative in a complex trickster tale. Lapin (Rabbit) and, to a lesser extent, Fox exhibit the characteristics of the virtually universal amoral trickster driven by his whims who bounces back from misfortune to win in the end. Rabbit (or Hare) plays the trickster role in Africa, African America, Europe, and Native America, and it is possible that any or all of these regions' traditions may have contributed to the following tale. Fox also is a cross-cultural character, appearing in both African American and European trickster tales. The story of the "Marriage of Compair Lapin," is enriched by the inclusion of Creole proverbs (indicated by **bold print***) and by an embedded folktale concerning the fate of messengers that reflects the ultimate fate of Bourriquet, King Lion's messenger. The opening passage of this tale alludes to "Compair Lapin and the Little Man of Tar."*

You all must remember, after they had thrown Compair Lapin into the briers, how quickly he had run away, saying that it was in those very thorns that his mother had made him. Now then, I will tell you that on the same day Miss Leonine went to meet him, and they started traveling. They walked a long time, for at least a month; at last they reached the bank of a river which was very deep. The current was strong, too strong for them to swim over. On the other side of the river there was a pretty place: the trees were green and loaded with all kinds of fruits. Under the trees were flowers of every kind that there is in the world. When a person breathed there, it was as if a bottle of essence had been opened in a room.

Miss Leonine said : "Let us go to live there; besides, we cannot return to my father's. There, we shall be happy, and no one will bother us; but how shall we do to cross over to the other side?"

"Stop," said Compair Lapin, "let me think a moment," and then he began to walk and walk, until he saw a large piece of dry wood which had fallen into the water. "That is what I want," said he. He cut a tall pole, and then he mounted on the log and told Leonine to follow him. Poor Miss Leonine mounted also, but she was so much afraid that she was trembling dreadfully.

"Hold on well; you will see how we shall pass," and he pushed with his stick. The log began to go down the current; they were going like lightning, and Lapin kept on paddling.

They sailed for half a day before they were able to reach the other side, for the current was so strong that the log was carried along all the time. At last it passed very near the shore. "Jump, jump," said Compair Lapin, and hardly had he spoken than he was on shore. Miss Leonine finally jumped also, and they found themselves on the other side of the river. They were very glad, and the first thing they did was to eat as much as they could of the good things they found there. Then they took a good rest.

They found a pretty place to pass the night, and the next day, at dawn, they took a good walk. As everything they saw was so fine, they thought they would remain there to live. When they had run away, they had not been able to take any money with them, so they were without a cent. But God had blessed them, for they had come to a place where they did not need much money. They had already been there a good while, and they were quiet and contented, and they thought that they were alone, when one day, they heard, all at once, a noise, a tumult, as if thunder was rolling on the ground.

"What is that, my lord? Go to see, Compair Lapin."

"I, no, as if I am foolish to go, and then catch something bad. It is better for me to stay quiet, and, in that way, nothing can happen to me."

The noise kept on increasing, until they saw approaching a procession of elephants. As they were passing quietly without attacking anyone, it gave Compair Lapin a little courage. He went to the chief of the elephants and told him that he asked his permission to remain in his country; he said that he came from the country of King Lion, who had wanted to kill him, and he had run away with his wife.

The elephant replied, "That is good; you may remain here as long as you want, but don't you bring here other animals who know how to eat one another. As long as you will behave well, I will protect you, and nobody will come to get you here. Come sometimes to see me, and I will try to do something for you."

Some time after that, Compair Lapin went to see the king of elephants, and the king was so glad when Compair Lapin explained to him how he could make a great deal of money, that he named immediately Compair Lapin captain of his bank and watchman of his property. When Compair Lapin saw all the money of the king it almost turned his head, and as he had taken the habit of drinking since they had dug in his country a well, of which the water made people drunk, he continued his bad habit whenever he had the chance.

One evening he came home very drunk, and he began quarrelling with his wife. Leonine fell upon him and gave him such a beating that he remained in bed for three weeks. When he got up, he asked his wife to pardon him. He said that he was drunk, and that he would never do it again, and he kissed her. In his heart, however, he could not forgive Leonine. He swore that he would leave her, but before that he was resolved to give her a terrible beating.

One evening when Leonine was sleeping, Compair Lapin took a rope and tied her feet before and behind. In that way he was sure of his business. Then he took a good whip, and he whipped her until she lost consciousness. Then he left her and went on traveling. He wanted to go to a place where they would never hear of him any more, because he was afraid that Leonine would kill him, and he went far.

When Miss Leonine came back to herself, she called, she called, they came to see what was the matter, and they found her well tied up. They cut the ropes, and Leonine started immediately. She left her house, she traveled a long time, until she came to the same river which she had crossed with Compair Lapin upon the log. She did not hesitate, but jumped into the water. The current carried her along, and she managed, after a great many efforts, to cross over to the other side. She was very tired, and she had to take some rest; then she started to return to her father.

When her father saw her, he kissed her and caressed her, but his daughter began to cry, and told him how Compair Lapin had treated her. When King Lion heard that, he was so angry that all who were near him began to tremble. "Come here, Master Fox; you shall go to the king of elephants, and tell him, that if he does not send Compair Lapin to me as soon as he can, I shall go to his country to kill him and all the elephants, and all the other animals, and everything which is in his country. Go quick."

Master Fox travelled a long time, an arrived at last in the country where Compair Lapin was hidden. But he did not see him; he asked for him, but no one could give him any news of him. Master Fox went to see the king of elephants and told him what King Lion had said. The elephants hate the lions, so the king replied, "Tell your master that if he wishes me to break his jaw-bone, let him come. I shall not send anything or anybody, and first of all, get away from here quick. If you want good advice, I can tell you that you had better remain in your country. If ever Lion tries to come here, I shall receive him in such a manner that no one of you will ever return home."

Master Fox did not wait to hear any more; but he had no great desire to go back to his country, for he thought Lion would kill him if he returned without Compair Lapin. He walked as slowly as he could, and all along the road he saw that they were making preparations for war. He thought that perhaps the elephants were going to attack King Lion. He went on his way, and on arriving at a prairie he saw Compair Lapin, who was running in zigzags, sometimes on one side of the road, sometimes on the other. He stopped whenever he met animals and spoke to them, and then he started again as rapidly as before. At last Master Fox and Compair Lapin met, but the latter did not recognize his old friend.

"Where are you going like that, running all the time?"

"Ah!" replied Compair Lapin, "you don't know the bad news. Lion has declared war against all elephants, and I want to notify all mules, horses, and camels to get out of the way."

"But you, why are you running so? They are surely not going to make a soldier of you?"

"No, you believe that. Ah, well, with all your cunning you know nothing. When the officers of the king will come to get the horses and mules for the cavalry to go to war, they will say: 'That's a fellow with long ears; he is a mule; let us take him.' Even if I protest, and say that I am a rabbit, they will say: 'Oh, no! Look at his ears; you see that he is a mule,' and I should be caught, enlisted, and forced to march. It seems to me that I know you, but it is such a long time since I have seen you. May God help me, it is Master Fox, my old friend!"

"Yes, yes, it is I, my good fellow. Well! what do you say about all that bad business?"

"All that is for a woman," said Compair Lapin; "we must try, my friend, to have nothing to do with that war."

"But what shall we do?" said Master Fox. "They will force us into it."

"No, you must be King Lion's adviser, and I will be that of King Elephant, and in that way we shall merely look on and let them fight as much as they want."

"You know," said Master Fox, "Leonine has returned to her father; and as you were not married before the church, I believe that Lion is about to marry her to one of his neighbors. Does it not grieve you, Compair Lapin, to think of that?"

"Oh, no; **we feel no sorrow for what we do not see.**"

The two cunning fellows conversed a long time, for they were glad to meet after such a long absence. As they were about to part, they saw two dogs, that stood nose to nose, growling fiercely, and then turned around rapidly and began to smell each other everywhere.

"You, Master Fox, who know everything, can you tell me why dogs have the bad habit of smelling each other in that way?"

"I will tell you, Compair Lapin, why they do that. In old, old times, when there was but one god, called Mr. Jupiter, all the dogs considered their lot so hard and unhappy that they sent a delegation to ask Mr. Jupiter to better their condition. When they arrived at the house of the god in heaven, all the dogs were so frightened that they ran away. Only one remained; it was Brisetout, the largest dog of the party. He was not afraid of anything, and he came to Mr. Jupiter, and spoke thus: 'My nation sent me to see you to ask you whether you think that we are going to watch over our masters all day and all night, bark all the time, and then be kicked right and left and have nothing to eat. We are too unhappy, and we want to know if you will allow us once in a while to eat one of the sheep of our masters. We cannot work like this for nothing. What do you say, Mr. Jupiter?'"

"'Wait a moment; I shall give you such a reply that you will never wish to annoy me any more. I am tired of hearing all sorts of complaints. I am tired, do you hear?'"

"Then Mr. Jupiter spoke a language that no one could understand, and one of his clerks went out to get something. He told the dog to sit down. Brisetout remained on the last step of the staircase. He thought that Mr. Jupiter was going to give him a good dinner; but the first thing he knew, the clerk returned with another man. They took hold of Brisetout, they tied him well, then they took a tin pan in which they put red pepper and turpentine. They rubbed the dog all over with the mixture; it burnt him so much that he howled and bellowed. When they let him go, Mr. Jupiter told him, 'You will give my reply to your comrades, and each one that will come to complain will be received in the same manner; you hear?'"

"Ah, no, Brisetout did not hear; he ran straight ahead without knowing where he was going. At last he arrived at a bayou, fell into it, and was drowned.

"Some time after that, Mr. Jupiter did not feel well. He thought he would leave heaven and take a little trip to earth. On his way he saw an apple tree which was covered with beautiful apples. He began to eat some, and while he was eating, a troop of dogs came to bark at him. Mr. Jupiter ordered his stick to give them a good drubbing. The stick began to turn to the right and to the left, and beat the dogs so terribly, that they scattered about in a minute. There remained but one poor dog, who was all mangy. He begged the stick to spare him. Then Stick pushed him before Mr. Jupiter, and said, 'Master, that dog was so thin that I did not have the courage to beat him.' 'It is very well,' said Mr. Jupiter, 'let him go; but if ever any dog comes to bark at me again, I shall destroy them all. I don't want to be bothered by you, I say. You have already sent me a delegation, and I received them so well that I don't think they will like to come back to see me. Have you already forgotten that?' The poor lean dog replied, 'What you say is true, but we never saw again the messenger we sent you; we are still waiting for him.' Mr. Jupiter then said, 'I will tell you how you can find out the messenger you had sent to me: let all dogs smell one another, and the one which will smell of turpentine is the messenger.'"

"You see now, Compair Lapin, why dogs smell one another. It was all Mr. Jupiter's doing. Poor old fellow, he has now lost all his clients, since the Pope ordered everybody to leave him, and he has had to close his shop. He left the heaven, and no one knows where he went to hide. You understand, Compair Lapin, people get tired of having always the same thing; so they took another religion, and I think that the one we have now is good."

"Thank you, thank you, Master Fox, for your good story; and in order to show you that I am your old friend, I will tell you what we can do. As I told you already, we must remain very quiet. As the elephants want to go to attack King Lion in his own country, they will make a bridge for the army to pass. When the bridge will be finished they will go straight ahead, without stopping anywhere, to attack King Lion, for they want to take him by surprise. Don't you tell that to anybody, you hear."

Compair Lapin and Master Fox then shook hands, and they parted. Master Fox went on his way, and Compair Lapin went to the king of elephants and asked him to give orders to all the carpenters and blacksmiths in the country to obey him. When all the workmen were assembled, Compair Lapin began to make the bridge, and soon finished it. On the side of the river which was in the country of the elephants, he made at the end of the bridge a large park. These were bars of iron planted in the earth; they were at least ten feet high, and so sharp that a fly could not touch one without being pierced through. Compair Lapin then covered the bars of iron with branches and brambles to make it appear like a patch of briers, in order that they might not know that it was a snare. Then he took four cows with their calves, and tied them in the very middle of the pit. Then he put in it red pepper, ashes, and tobacco snuff. Then he placed in the trap a great number of tubs of water, in which there was a drug that made people go to sleep right off. After he had finished all this, Compair Lapin said, "Now let King Lion come to attack us."

Master Fox was still traveling to render an account of his errand to King Lion, but he was so much afraid to return without Compair Lapin, that he concluded that it was better not to return at all. On his way he met a hen; he killed it, and covered an old rag with the blood. He tied his hind paw with the rag, and he began to limp, and jump on three feet. At last he met Bourriquet (Donkey), to whom he said : "My dear friend, render me a little service; you see how sick I am. I pray you to go to King Lion, to tell him that I cannot come to see him. The elephants broke my leg because I had come to claim Compair Lapin."

"Oh, no!" said Bourriquet; "you were always against me with Compair Lapin. Go yourself."

"That is good," said Master Fox ; "**I shall have my chance again, you will need me again.** If you knew what I have seen and what I know, you would listen to me."

"Well, tell me all," said Bourriquet; "and I will go, since you cannot walk."

"That is all right; listen well. The elephants intend to come to attack King Lion in his country. They are making a bridge to cross the river, and as soon as the bridge will be finished they will come immediately to surprise Lion. If the king understood his business, he would hasten to attack the elephants in their own country, before they come to lift him up before he knows it."

As soon as Master Fox had finished speaking, Bourriquet galloped away and went to King Lion, to whom he said what Master Fox had related to him. The king was so glad that he ordered someone to give Bourriquet a little hay to eat. Bourriquet was not very much pleased, and he began grumbling.

"Don't you know, Bourriquet," said the king's servant, "that you must not look at the bridle of a horse which was given to you."

"Well," said Bourriquet, "I had expected a better reward, but I'll take that anyhow, because **a bird in the hand is better than two in the bush.**"

All at once they heard a dreadful noise. It was King Lion, who was starting for the war with all the animals which he could find: tigers, bears, wolves, all King Lion's subjects were there. As to Master Fox, he had run back to notify Compair Lapin that the enemies were coming.

Miss Leonine was with the army, and her father used to tell her all the time, "I am glad that you came; Compair Lapin will have to pay for all his tricks; you must treat him as he treated you."

King Lion was at the head of the army, and coming near the bridge he saw Master Fox, who was lying in the road with his leg broken.

"Oh! Oh!" said Lion, "this is the way they treated you! They shall have to pay for all that."

"Make haste," said Master Fox; "don't wait till they come to attack you; pass the bridge immediately; that will throw them in confusion."

The army went on. They all ran to pass over the bridge, King Lion at the head, with his daughter. As soon as they arrived at the place where was the snare, and they saw the cows and their calves, King Lion and his troops killed them and began to eat them. Then they quarreled among themselves and began to fight. They scattered about the ashes, the red pepper, and the tobacco snuff, and were completely blinded. They fought terribly; they massacred one another; then those that were left drank the water in the tubs. Two hours later they were all sound asleep.

The elephants, which had remained prudently at a distance, hearing no more noise, came to the bridge. They killed all the animals that were left in Lion's army, and threw their bodies in the river. They flayed King Lion; they took his skin and sewed Bourriquet into it ; then they tied some straw, covered with pitch, to Bourriquet's tail; they put fire to the straw, and they let him go to announce the news in Lion's country.

When Bourriquet passed on the bridge, he was galloping so fast that one might have thought that it was thunder that was rolling on the bridge, as if it were more than one hundred cart loads. When Bourriquet arrived in his country his tail was entirely consumed by the fire, but he said that he had lost it in a battle. Although he announced very sad news, no one could help laughing at him: he was so funny without his tail, and so proud of his glorious wound.

As soon as all was over at the bridge, Compair Lapin went to get Master Fox, and took him to the king of the elephants. He presented him to his majesty, and told him that Master Fox was his good friend, and if the king wanted to accept his services, they would both be his very faithful subjects.

The king of elephants said to them "I believe that you are two cunning rascals, and that in my war with King Lion, Master Fox **had been on both**

sides of the fence, but all right, he may remain here, if he wants. As for you, Compair Lapin, I want you to get married. Here is Miss White Rabbit; she is rich, and will be a good match for you. Tomorrow I want to dance at the wedding."

The next day all the people assembled, and celebrated with great splendor the marriage of Compair Lapin with Miss White Rabbit. Master Fox was the first groomsman. Three weeks after the wedding, Mrs. Compair Lapin gave birth to two little ones; one was white and the other as black as soot. Compair Lapin was not pleased, and he went to see the king of elephants.

"Oh! you know nothing," said the king; "you are married before the church, and I will not grant you a divorce. Besides, I must tell you that in the family of Mrs. Compair Lapin it happens very often that the little ones are black. It is when the ladies are afraid in a dark night; so console yourself, and don't be troubled."

Compair Lapin consented to remain with his wife until death should part them, and that is how he married after all his pranks.

As I was there when all that happened, I ran away to relate it to you.

Source: Adapted from "The Marriage of Compair Lapin," Alcée Fortier. *Louisiana Folk-Tales* (Boston & New York, American Folk-Lore Society, 1895), pp. 39–53.

Rabbit Rides Wolf

The Native American Creek Confederacy had extensive contact includ-ing intermarriage with the French from at least the early eighteenth century, and with Africans and African Americans since the beginning of the Southern slave trade. For example, Rosa Parks (1913–2005), labeled by the United States Congress as the "Mother of the Modern-Day Civil Rights Movement," was of African and Creek descent. The following Creek tale represents another impressive example of the mutual influence among African, European, and Native American folklore; the fact that variations of this tale appear in the folktale reper-toires of all three groups should come as no surprise.

Some girls lived not far from Rabbit and Wolf, and Rabbit thought he would like to visit them. So one time he called upon Wolf and said, "Let us go visiting." Wolf said, "All right," and they started off. When they got to the place the girls told them to sit down and they took a great liking to Wolf, who had a good time with them while Rabbit had to sit by and look on. Of course he was not pleased at this turn of affairs and said presently, "We had better be going back." But Wolf replied, "Let us wait a while longer," and they remained until it was late.

Before they left Rabbit got a chance to speak to one of the girls so that Wolf would not overhear and he said, "The one you are having so much sport with is my old horse." "I think you are lying," said the girl. "I am not. You shall see me ride him up here tomorrow." "If we see you ride him up we'll believe you."

When they started off the girls said, "Well, call again." Wolf was anxious to do so and early next morning be called upon Rabbit, whose house was much nearer, and said, "Are we going?" "I was sick all night," Rabbit answered, "and I hardly feel able to go." Wolf urged him, but he said at first that be really wasn't able to. Finally, however, he said, "If you will let me ride you I might go along just for company." So Wolf agreed to carry him astride of his back. But then Rabbit said, "I would like to put a saddle on you so as to brace myself," and Wolf agreed to it. "I believe it would be better," added Rabbit, "if I should bridle you." Wolf did not like this idea but Rabbit said, "Then I could hold on better and manage to get there," so Wolf finally consented to be bridled. Finally Rabbit wanted to put on spurs. Wolf replied, "I am too ticklish," but Rabbit said, "I will not spur you with them. I will hold them away from you but it would be nicer to have them on," so Wolf finally agreed, saying only, "I am very ticklish; you must not spur me." "When we got near the house," said Rabbit, "we will take everything off of you and walk the rest of the way."

So Rabbit and Wolf started on, but when they were nearly in sight of the house Rabbit plunged the spurs into Wolf and before he knew it they had passed right by the house. Then Rabbit said, "They have seen you now. I will tie you here and go up to see them and come back after a while and let you go." So Rabbit went to the house and said to the girls, "You all saw it, did you not?" "Yes," they answered, and he sat down and had a good time with them.

After a while Rabbit thought he ought to let Wolf go and started back to the place where he was fastened. He knew that Wolf was angry with him and thought up a way by which he could loose him with safety to himself. First he found a thin hollow log which he beat upon as if it were a drum. Then he ran up to Wolf as fast as he could go and cried out, "Do you know they are hunting for you? You heard the drum just now. The soldiers are after you." Wolf was very much frightened and said "Let me go." Rabbit was purposely a little slow in untying him and he had barely gotten him freed when Wolf broke away and went off as fast as he could run. Then Rabbit returned to the house and remained there as if he were already a married man.

Near this house was a large peach orchard and one day Rabbit said to the girls, "I will shake the peaches off for you." So they all went to the orchard together and he climbed up into a tree to shake the peaches off. While he was there Wolf came toward them and called out, "Old fellow, I am not going to let you alone." By that time he was almost under the tree. Then Rabbit shouted out loud as if to people at a distance, "Here is that fellow for whom you are always hunting," and Wolf ran away again.

Some time after this, while Rabbit was lying close under a tree bent over near the ground, he saw Wolf coming. Then he stood up with the tree extended over his shoulder as if he were trying to hold it up. When Wolf saw him he said, "I have you now." Rabbit, however, called out, "They told me to hold this tree up all day with the great power I have and for it they would give me four hogs. I don't like hog meat but you do, so you might get it if you take my place," Wolf's greed was excited by this and he was willing to hold up the tree. Then Rabbit said, "If you yield only a little it will give way, so you must hold it tight." And he ran off. Wolf stood under the tree so long that finally he felt he could stand it no longer and he jumped away quickly so that it would not fall upon him. Then he saw that it was a growing tree rooted in the earth. "That Rabbit is the biggest liar," he exclaimed, "if I can catch him I will certainly fix him."

After that Wolf hunted about for Rabbit once more and finally came upon him in a nice grassy place. He was about to spring upon him when Rabbit said, "My friend, don't punish me. I have food for you. There is a horse lying out yonder." Wolf's appetite was again moved at the prospect and he decided to go along. Then Rabbit said, "It is pretty close to a house, therefore it would be well for me to tie your tail to the horse's tail so that you can drag it off to a place where you can feast at leisure." So Rabbit tied the two tails together. But the horse was only asleep, not dead, as Wolf "supposed," and Rabbit ran around to its head and kicked it. At once the horse jumped up and was so frightened that it kicked and kicked until it kicked Wolf to death.

Source: Adapted from "Myths and Tales of the Southeastern Indians." John R. Swanton (Washington, DC: Smithsonian Institution. Bureau of American Ethnology. Bulletin 88. U.S. Government Printing Office. 1929), 64–66.

Brother Rabbit, Brother Booky, and Brother Cow

Booky (spelled variously as Bouki, Bouqui, Booky, Buki, from the Wolof word for "hyena") and Rabbit (Brother Rabbit, Compair Lapin) are commonly paired in African American narrative: in the Southeastern United States, in French Creole regions, and in the Caribbean. In most cases, Booky plays the foil to Rabbit, the clever trickster, and is the butt of all Rabbit's jokes. See, for example, "The Elephant and the Whale." In this tale from the Bahamas, however, Booky imitates Rabbit, tries his hand at being a con man, triumphs over his targets and wins Rabbit's praise. A similar tale featuring Compair Lapin and Bouki is found in Louisiana in which a smokehouse filled with hams is raided.

Once it was a time, a very good time,
De monkey chewed tobacco an' 'e spit white lime

Now on this day Brother Rabbit and Brother Booky were together. The wind was blowin'; they didn' t have nothin' to eat; they couldn't catch no fish. They was travelin' along to see if they couldn't find something to eat. An' now when Brother Rabbit look he saw one big cow. He went over to the cow.

Then he take his hand an' spank on the cow bottom. he say, "Open, Kabendye [magical phrase], open!" When the cow bottom open, Brother Rabbit jumped in with his knife an' his pan. He cut on the inside of the cow until his pan was full of meat. Brother Rabbit said, "Open, Kabendye, open!" and the cow bottom open an' Brother Rabbit jumped out.

Good! Now Brother Rabbit was goin' home; his pan full o' meat. Brother Booky see Brother Rabbit and said, "Brother Rabbit, where you get all that meat?" Brother Booky say, "If you don't tell me where you get all that meat I'm goin' to tell everybody what you got!"

Brother Rabbit said, "Go right down there where you see one big cow."

Brother Booky said, "All right!"

Brother Rabbit and the Bag of Gold

In the following tale Rabbit, using a ploy reminiscent of Tom Sawyer's fence painting scheme, connives to get his neighbors to take on the work of constructing a spring house (a small storage shed built over a spring in order to keep food cold). In this case, Rabbit reveals that he is not only clever but also extraordinarily lucky.

You've heard how Brother Rabbit's left foot will fetch you luck when you tote it constantly in your pocket. It most surely does that, 'cause that Old Brother Rabbit was just born to luck. Now this here is one time when the luck came to himself.

Old Miss Rabbit, she decided that she was determined to have a spring house; she said, Old Miss Rabbit did, how Miss Fox and Miss Coon have the nice spring house, and she declared that she was plumb broke down worrying herself trying to keep house, and no spring house.

Now Brother Rabbit, he promised and he promised, but Brother Rabbit don't have no hankering to handle the mattocks, that he don't. Brother Rabbit is powerful dexterous to work with his head, but Brother Rabbit ain't got no hankering to work with his hands.

But Old Miss Rabbit, she kept worrying the old man constantly; she demanded that she was obliged to have that spring house, and she was obliged to have it at once.

Well, when she reared and charged on the old man, so powerful that he can't put her off no more, then Brother Rabbit, he just went off to himself, and thought about what he was going do about that ornery old spring house, but he can't see any way around doing what she wanted, until it came to his mind about Old Mammy Witch Wise, her what was the old woman that save up a bag of gold. Then, the night before she die, she buried the bag where the critters can't find it. That night she passed by all the critters' houses and shook the bag, and they heard the clink of the gold, and in the morning Old Mammy Witch Wise was dead and the gold was gone.

Well, Brother Rabbit he went and he saw all the critters, and he let out the news how he done have a token that tell him where Old Mammy Witch Wise buried the gold, and that Old Brother Rabbit, he bodaciously told about how the token pointed to the bed in the spring that run along side his garden, and he said, Brother Rabbit did, if they all turned up and helped to make a dam and hold the water back, they would most surely find the gold.

Now Old Brother Rabbit don't have no feelings that gold was anywhere in them parts. Well, the critters they thought to themselves Brother Rabbit is a mighty generous man to let them in, and they fetched their mattocks and their spades, and they dug, and Brother Rabbit he sat up on the dam and located the spot, and he said to himself that old spring house getting built mighty fast, when I declare before the Lord, Brother Wolf's mattocks strike kerchink, and out flew the gold, it most surely did, and the critters they just jumped in the hole and picked up the money. But Old Brother Rabbit never lost his head, that he didn't, and he just pushed the rocks out of the dam, and let the water rush on out and drown the lastest one of them critters, and then he picks up the gold, and of course Old Miss Rabbit done got her spring house, but bless your soul, that only just one they times when Old Brother Rabbit had luck.

Source: Adapted from "Rabbit Born to Luck, Tales of the Rabbit from Georgia Negroes." Emma M Backus. *Journal of American Folklore* 12 (1899): 108–115, pp. 111–112.

SOCIETY AND CONFLICT

Brother Fox and the Foolish Jay-Bird

The following narrative takes the form of a fable, a tale intended to teach a moral lesson that ends with a direct statement of the point of the story, usually in the form of a proverb. As is often the case in fables, animals display human characteristics in order to illustrate the penalties inherent in violating social rules. This type of tale enjoys worldwide distribution. Modern readers are most familiar with the form through the fables attributed to Aesop. The tale of "Brother Fox and the Foolish Jay-Bird" pits two trickster figures against each other with tragic results for the character who is too clever for his own good. Jay-bird's fate reveals the inevitable results of giving in to envy to the extent that one is led to strike self-destructive bargains.

One day Brother Fox been eating some Turkey, and he got a bone stuck in his tooth what made it mighty hot, and achy. It hurt so bad he can't eat nothing for four days, so he went to Mr. Jay-bird and asked him to pull the piece of bone out. Mr. Jay-bird agreed to pull it out; but the Jay-bird was a mighty cute and schemey bird, he was jealous of Mr. Mockingbird, because he was the finest singer, and he hated him because he mocked him. He made a plan in his mind to get Brother Fox to kill Mr. Mockingbird, and all his family, so Blue-jay agreed to pull out the piece of bone; but he made Brother Fox wait a long time first, whilst he told him how dangerous it was to chew big bones. Then when Brother Fox get mighty impatient, Blue-jay hopped on his jaw, and pecked the piece of bone out of his tooth. Brother Fox was mighty relieved.

"There Brother Fox!" he says, "that's all right. Now I'm going to give you some good advice: you eat little bones after this. If you have a mind to, just as soon as it gets dark, I'm going to show you where Mr. Mockingbird and his whole family roosts, and then you can catch him and taste meat that is sweet."

And with that he went on about how good bird bones taste, 'til Brother Fox mouth just watered. Then he asked, "You feel a heap better, don't you, Brother Fox?'' and Brother' Fox he say, sort of anxious-like, "I'm afraid you have left a little piece of that bone in there yet. I wish you would just step in again and look, Brother Jay-bird."

Then, when Mr. Jay-bird hopped on his jaw, to look in his tooth, Brother Fox snapped his mouth shut and caught him, and make this remark, through his teeth, "Yes, Mr. Jay-bird, I do feel a heap better; I feel so much better that I am hungry, and you told me so much about the fine flavor of the little bones, that I can't wait 'til night come, to try them!"

And with that he chewed him up, and said the flavor was very fine indeed.

When you bargain with a rascal to harm your friends, you better make sure you are in a safe place yourself before you begin to make your agreement.

Source: Adapted from "Bro' Fox and de Foolish Jay-Bird," Emma M. Backus and Ethel Hatton Leitner. "Negro Tales from Georgia," *The Journal of American Folklore* 25 (1912): 125–136, pp. 127–128.

Brother Rabbit Brings Brother Fox
Back from the Dead

Brother Rabbit and Brother Fox, the two supreme tricksters of African American folktales, are commonly pitted against each other. As usual, Brother Rabbit proves himself to be more clever than Brother Fox. Not only does Fox's immediate plot backfire, but he loses face in the community permanently.

Brother Rabbit and Brother Fox were courting the Possum gal. Brother Rabbit was a mighty smooth-talking chap among the gals, and he had the gals nigh about all to himself. All you heard from the gals was, "Mr. Rabbit this, and Mr. Rabbit that," and the balance of the chaps had to stand back.

One night Brother Fox he go up to pay his respects to the Possum gal, and the servant fetched down word to him that Miss Possum had a previous engagement, and Brother Fox he just naturally knew Brother Rabbit was sitting up in the parlor with Miss Possum, and Brother Fox he just' can't stand it. He pondered, Brother Fox do, how he was going to send Brother Rabbit home. Now Brother Rabbit was a doctor. Brother Rabbit was a right good doctor, sure enough.

So now Brother Fox he went home, and he made like he had a fit and died, and he stretched himself out on the floor like he plum dead. Miss Fox and the little Foxes they rushed around and cried and they said, "Send for the doctor! Send for the doctor!"

So the little Fox boy he took off as hard as he can run for the doctor. He knocked at Miss Possum's door; he said, "Where is the doctor? A man's dead, and they done sent me for the doctor."

And Brother Rabbit he asked, "Who is dead?" And when the little Fox boy said it was Brother Fox, Brother Rabbit he don't want to go, but Miss Possum she took on so. She called Brother Rabbit a cruel man, so Brother Rabbit he put on his hat and lit out for Brother Fox's house.

When Brother Rabbit got to Brother Fox's house, sure enough he finds Brother Fox stretched out and looking like he is plum dead, but Brother Rabbit he had his suspicions. He felt of Brother Fox's heart. It was right warm. Then Brother Rabbit he said, "I never believe nobody is dead 'til I hear them give a big groan."

Brother Fox he gave a monstrous powerful groan "Ounk!"

Then Brother Rabbit he just kicked Brother Fox, and called him "a deceitful old man," and Brother Rabbit he lit back out to Miss Possum's house. Brother Rabbit he told Miss Possum about Brother Fox's mean, deceitful ways. From that time, when Miss Possum meet Brother Fox on the big road, she made like she don't know him, and she favored Brother Rabbit more than she ever had before.

Source: Adapted from "When Brer Fox Don't Fool Brer Rabbit," Emma M. Backus. "Folktales from Georgia," *Journal of American Folklore* 13 (1900): 19–32, pp. 24–25.

Dog and Dog-Head

The irony of Frog's deceiving the master trickster, Rabbit, gives this story an unusual twist. The trips to London to buy and sell goods suggests the influence of European tales. Many variations of the tale have been found in Jamaica and in the American South, but there seem to be no similar tales in Africa. This suggests that this is a plot that arose in comparatively recent times in the Western Hemisphere.

The rabbit and the frog were partners, and they were living on the same plantation. They had raised some rice, and were going to London with it. So, they sacked it up and got ready to start.

The rabbit could travel faster than the frog, so he would stop once in a while to wait for the frog. "Brother Frog, can't you come no faster than that?" said Brother Rabbit.

"You just go on, Brother Rabbit, I'll be there," said the frog.

"Yes, I know you will when you eat up all the rice," said Brother Rabbit. The rabbit thought that the frog was eating the rice because the frog panted under his throat, and the rabbit thought he was chewing.

"Well," said the rabbit, "I ask to eat some of mine, too. You will not eat all our rice and be fat, and me be poor." So the rabbit began to eat, and ate till he ate almost all his share of the rice.

Later on, they both wanted to buy a hound, so they could catch a deer. When they got to London, the frog had enough to buy him a hound, but the rabbit had just enough to buy him a dog's head. On the way back home the frog's dog jumped a deer and caught it. The frog could not keep up with the dog, but the rabbit he kept up and did the tracking. When the dog caught the deer, Brother Rabbit ran the frog's dog away, and put his dog head there by the deer.

When the frog got there, Brother Rabbit said, "Brother Frog, I thought your dog was worth something, but that there dog head of mine he can fly. Just look how he stuck to that deer and caught it! Your old dog was scared to go there. Hold him dog head! Don't let him go!"

"Now, Brother Frog, you go over there where you see that fire is at and get some fire, and I will give you half the deer." They saw the moon rising, and they thought it was a fire. Brother Frog went hopping just as fast as he could. Soon as he thought he was far enough so that the rabbit could not see him, he hopped behind a large tree for a while and soon came back.

Frog said, "Brother Rabbit, that man would not let me have no fire."

Then Brother Rabbit looked in the west and saw a star. "Well, yonder is another man with some fire; go over there."

Away Brother Frog went, but soon came back again. "Brother Rabbit, that man say for you to come. I walk too slow." Away Brother Rabbit went, leaving Brother Frog to watch till he come back.

Brother Rabbit soon came again. "Brother Frog, that man lives too far away."

"Well, Brother Rabbit, just go right back over there to that man, he don't live very far. You can go there."

"Brother Frog, you ought to go, for somebody might take that deer away from you."

"No, they won't, neither! I'm a man, a good man, too," said Brother Frog. So Brother Rabbit went again.

While Brother Rabbit was gone, Brother Frog hid the deer so Brother Rabbit could not see him. Then he went jumping up and scream and hollered and called," Brother Rabbit, Brother Rabbit!"

Brother Rabbit came running. "What's the matter? What's the matter? "

"A great big red-eyed man came and took that deer away from me."

"Look here Brother Frog, you say his eyes was red?"

"Yes, his eyes was red," Brother Frog he said.

"Well, I don't care about that deer anyhow," said Brother Rabbit. "Any old fool ought to know an old dead dog head can't catch no deer. Your old dog caught him. I just was making a fool out you."

"Brother Rabbit, I knowed that you was lying. I carried that deer home. I knowed my dog caught that deer. I ain't going to give you a bit, neither. Now you go along to your house. I'll go to mine." And away they both went.

Source: Adapted from "Dog and Dog Head," A.M. Bacon. and Elsie Clews Parsons. "Folk-Lore from Elizabeth City County, Virginia," *Journal of American Folklore* 35 (1922): 250–327, pp. 269–270.

Compair Lapin and the Earthworm

Trickster tales are commonly cyclical; individual tales of single exploits are linked together around the stock character of clever rascals such as Tortoise, Fox, Coyote, or Rabbit. "Compair Lapin and the Earthworm" illustrates one of the ways in which cycles are constructed through alluding to events that occurred in the narrative "The Elephant and the Whale." The worm who threatens Compair Lapin is not an earthworm, but Cuterebra, the inch-long larvae of the botfly. These larvae burrow into rabbits' skins, especially around the neck and jaw area, and can, if left untreated, cause death.

Everybody knows that every year in the month of May Compair Lapin is sick; it is an earthworm which is in his neck, biting him and sucking his blood like a leech. That makes him weak, weak, and for a month the worm holds on to him, hooked in his neck, before it falls. Rabbits believe that when they lie down in the grass the worms come out of the grass and climb on them. They are, therefore, very much afraid of worms, and if they see one, they run as if they had a pack of hounds after them. If I tell you that it is because I want to relate to you a story about Compair Lapin and the worm.

It was a day in spring, the little birds were singing, the butterflies were flying about from one flower to another. It seemed as if all animals were rendering thanks to God for his kindness to them. A little earthworm was the only one which was crying and complaining. He said he was so small, he had neither feet, nor hands, nor wings, and was obliged to remain in his hole. The little birds, the lizards, and even the ants were troubling him and eating his little ones. If God would make him big and strong, like other animals, then he would be contented, because he would be able to defend himself, while now he was helpless in his hole. He cried and cried and said that he would be glad if he belonged to the Devil. Hardly had he spoken when he saw the Devil at his side.

"Well, I heard all you said; tell me what you want; I shall grant it to you, and you will belong to me when you die."

"What I want? Yes. I want strength, I want to become big, big, and beat everybody who will come to trouble and bother me. Give me only that and I shall be satisfied."

"That is all right," said the Devil; "let me go, in a short while you will be contented."

As soon as the Devil had gone, the worm found himself strong and big. The change had come suddenly, and his hole had become large and as deep as a well. The worm was so glad that he began to laugh and to sing. At that very moment Lapin passed, and he was terribly frightened. He ran until he was unable to go any farther, and, when he stopped, he whistled, "fouif." "Never," said he, "was I more frightened. I shall never sleep again as long as that big earthworm will remain in this country. If I had not been so foolish as to boast that I could beat the elephant, I should go to him. It is Bouki who told on me; but perhaps if I speak to him I shall be able ma to fix up matters. I must try to make them meet and fight, and perhaps I shall get rid of both at the same time. It would be a pretty fight. Let me go and see the elephant, or I won't be able to sleep tonight. Besides, the earthworm said that he would fix me. I can't live that way. Good gracious! What am I to do? Let me arrange in my head what I am going to tell the elephant in order to please him."

He went on until he met the elephant. He bowed very politely, and the elephant did likewise, and asked him how he was.

"Oh! I am very sick," said Compair Lapin; "another time I shall come to try my strength with you; I think I can beat you."

"You are a fool," said the elephant. "Go away, I don't want to harm you; I take pity on you."

"I bet you," said Compair Lapin, "that I can beat you."

"All right, whenever you want."

"A little later; but as I know that you are good, I had come to ask you a favor."

"What is it?"

"It is to help me, to give me a hand to carry lumber to build my cabin."

"Let us go right off, if you want."

Compair Lapin, who had carried his axe with him, cut down a big tree, and said to the elephant: "Take it by the big end, I shall raise the branches, and we shall carry the tree to the place where I wish to build my cabin."

The elephant put the tree on his shoulder without looking behind him, and Compair Lapin climbed into the branches, and let the elephant do all the work. When the latter was tired he would stop to rest a little, and Compair Lapin would jump down and run up to the elephant to encourage him. "How is that, Compair, you are already tired; but that is nothing. Look at me, who have been working as much as you. I don't feel tired."

"What! That is mightily heavy," said the elephant.

"Let us go," said Lapin; "we have not far to go."

The big animal put the load again on his back and Compair Lapin appeared to be lifting the branches. Whenever the elephant would not be looking Lapin would sit on a branch and say, "A little farther; go to the right, go to the left."

At last they came to the hole of the earthworm, and Lapin told the elephant to put down the tree. He let it fall right upon the worm who was sleeping. The latter pushed out the tree as if it were a piece of straw, and coming out he began to insult the elephant. Compair Lapin went to hide in a place where he could see and hear all. The elephant lost patience and struck the worm with his trunk.

The worm then climbed up the back of the elephant, and there was a terrible fight for more than two hours, until they were nearly dead. The worm finally hid in his hole and the elephant lay down dying. Compair Lapin mounted upon him, pulled his ears and beat him, and said to him, "Didn't I tell you I would beat you?"

"Oh! yes, Compair Lapin; I have enough; I am dying."

Lapin then left him, and, going into the worm's hole, be broke his head with a stick. "Now," said he, "I am rid of both of them."

A little later Compair Lapin met Compair Bouki and told him how he had made the elephant and the earthworm fight until they had killed one another. "You see, my friend, when two fellows are in your way, you must make them fight, then you will always save your skin."

Source: Adapted from "Compair Lapin and the Earthworm," Alcée Fortier. *Louisiana Folk-Tales* (Boston & New York: American Folk-Lore Society, 1895), pp. 13–19.

Sis 'Coon Shows Brother 'Coon Who's the Boss

The following narrative examines the true basis of power in social relationships. Bear, who commonly represents physical strength coupled with mental weakness in African American folktales, intimidates children and their father by an ominous presence and verbal nonsense. Brother 'Coon (Raccoon), enforces his commands to Sis 'Coon by calling on the traditional husband-wife relationship: "Ain't you my wife? Well, you do like I tell you." His power to protect the family ultimately proves as empty of real substance as his basis for authority, and Sis 'Coon literally takes matters into her own hands, thus ending the threat and causing a power shift in the family.

Brother 'Coon and Sis 'Coon they had a mighty fine house up in the big woods. They were mighty good livers; poor, industrious people. They have right smart of children, and they leave the children every day, Brother 'Coon and Sis 'Coon do, and go to work soon in the morning.

Brother Bear he knows how Brother 'Coon and Sis 'Coon done leave the children and go to work soon every morning, and when Brother Bear's way lay past Brother 'Coon's house, Brother Bear he smell the good cooked victuals.

Now Brother Bear he know nobody ain't to home except the children, so Brother Bear he goes knocking on the door, and the children they say, "Who's there?

"Brother Bear he says in a heavy voice, "Revenue, Revenue, where's my hole? Revenue, Revenue, where's my hole?" And the little "Coon children," they all that frightened, they run up in the loft and hide, and Brother Bear he go in and eat up the every one of the victuals.

When Brother 'Coon and Sis 'Coon come home, they find the children frightened nigh about out of their senses, and all the victuals done gone. They blamed the children, and the children done told them how a big black thing done come and knocked on the door and said, "Revenue, Revenue, where's my hole? Revenue, Revenue, where's my hole?" and how he done eat up all the victuals.

Next day Brother Bear he came just the same, saying the same words in the same voice, and the children run and hide, and Brother Bear he ate up all the victuals.

That night Brother 'Coon and Sis 'Coon they talked about what they were going to do. Sis 'Coon she said how she was going to stay home and watch with the axe, and Brother 'Coon he said, Sis 'Coon go to work, and he going stay home himself and watch with the axe. Sis 'Coon she hold to how she going stay home; and Brother 'Coon he say, "Ain't you my wife? Well, you do like I tell you." So Sis 'Coon she was obliged to go to work, and Brother 'Coon he stayed home and watched with the axe in his hand.

Just as they get the table set for dinner, sure enough here comes a great black thing knocking at the door. Brother 'Coon he was powerful scared, but he called out, "Who's there?" Brother Bear he said in a mighty heavy voice, "Revenue, Revenue, where's my hole? Revenue, Revenue, where's my hole?" Brother 'Coon he gave one look at him and he dropped the axe right where he's at, and Brother 'Coon he just flew up in the loft, and the little 'Coon children they all fly up in the loft with their paw. Brother Bear he came in and ate up all the victuals.

When Sis 'Coon got home she found the family all hiding in the loft, and nothing in the house to eat, and when Brother 'Coon told her how the big black thing frighten him, Miss 'Coon she was scared. She said she don't want to stay home and watch.

Next morning Brother 'Coon he said he was going away to work, and Sis 'Coon she said she don' want to stay home and watch.

Brother 'Coon he said, "Ain't you my wife? Then you do like I tell you." So Brother 'Coon he goes off to work, and he leaves Sis 'Coon to watch with the axe.

Sure enough, just as soon as they get the table set for dinner, here come a great black thing knocking at the door. Sis 'Coon she said, "Who's there? "

Brother Bear he say in powerful gruff tone, "Revenue, Revenue, where's my hole ? Revenue, Revenue, where's my hole?"

Sis 'Coon she cracked the door, and when Brother Bear he stepped in, Sis 'Coon took the axe and split his head open.

And after that, Brother 'Coon he don't order Miss 'Coon around these days, but from that day on Brother 'Coon he done been a plum henpecked man.

Source: Adapted from "Folk-Tales from Georgia," Emma M. Backus. *Journal of American Folklore* 13 (1900): 19–32, pp. 26–27.

Owl and Blacksnake

*The following fable, like many tales of this type, uses animal charac-
ters who assume human behavior in order to teach a social lesson.
In addition, in keeping with the general pattern, the moral of the story
is summed up by a proverb put in the mouth of the victor in the strug-
gle between Owl and Blacksnake.*

In the old time not the very oldest, when all things were very friendly, Owl
and Blacksnake were not great favorites with the other creatures. In conse-
quence of this, they were to a great extent dependent on each other for
company, and many were the rehearsals of evil gossip they had, as they sat
together on a clay bank or the low, dry limb of some stunted tree. They
talked much, and always unkindly, of their neighbors. They were companions, but not friends, for whenever they met, each slyly tried to make the
other tell her secrets while withholding her own. They were both sorceresses
of great power and wickedness. Truly each was worthy to be the other's
only associate.

While they were plotting and planning together against their acquaint-
ances, and bringing bad luck to the harmless and unfortunate, they were
also secretly considering how they could do each other great wrong. Above
all things, Blacksnake wished for some owl eggs, for next to the hot and
quivering brains of a rat nothing could give more power for conjuring; but
she did not long for them more ardently than did Owl for a meal of snake
eggs. Owl was getting old and rheumatic, and had tried the ointment made
of black dog's grease without having her youthful suppleness and vivacity
restored. Only snake eggs could make her young and active once more.
The two talked and talked, and paid each other deceitful compliments, and
all the while they were burning and tingling to get at each other's nests.

One day Owl found her opportunity. Blacksnake had gone to a great
meadow of tall, rough grass to hunt young rats, for it was the season when
many were to be found, if one looked in the right place. Scarce had she
glided away when Owl, blinking in the dim light (it was a cloudy day, else
weak as her eyes were she could not have been out at all), came searching
about for the coveted "medicine." She soon found the eggs, tore open their

tough envelopes, and ate the "meat" with great satisfaction. This done, she flew away, saying to herself as she did so, "That is a great matter settled for me, and no one can ever know. Certainly, Blacksnake, if she has any suspicions, will fasten them on Weasel, or Ferret, or, perhaps, Gopher. Yes, she is likely to think that Gopher, stirring around where he was not wanted, destroyed them as readily from a love of mischief as the others would from the pleasure they have in sucking eggs."

Two things she had forgotten to wipe her foot as well as her mouth, and to consider that a fragment of shell can tell a tale better than a whole egg. While she was eating she had spilled a portion of the "egg-meat" and stepped in it. She did not notice that this left a print of her foot beside the rifled nest. The other silent witness was the shell. There were no tooth marks such as Weasel, or Ferret, or Gopher would make on its tough edges. Either bit of evidence was enough, but she flew away without reckoning on even one of them.

When Blacksnake went home she was almost brokenhearted. She could not at first discover any clue to the robber; her suspicions were confused and contradictory. When she became calmer she carefully examined the ground and found Owl's footprint. Then she became very quiet. She coiled herself up under some leaves and meditated on vengeance.

Next day Owl made a call, looking as innocent as she could. Blacksnake was not at home. Owl waited a little, but as Blacksnake did not return, she went home when the sun shone out.

The next evening, when her mate relieved her of the care of the nest, she went back. Still no Blacksnake!

A third and a fourth visit she made, and still Blacksnake did not make her appearance. Owl did not know whether to be relieved or doubly apprehensive. Either Blacksnake had grieved herself to death or she had gone into some secret place to work spells of divination or cursing. The case called for serious thought. Owl set out for home feeling very serious. As she passed an old hollow tree, on which she and Blacksnake had often held meetings, she heard a faint voice calling her name. The voice sounded from the large limbs, and evidently was Blacksnake's. In another moment the snake's head appeared at a knothole.

"Is that you, my cousin?" she called to Owl.

Owl feigned great delight at seeing her, and said "What can I do for you, dear Blacksnake? Truly, I have feared these last days that you were lost or killed."

"Almost have I died," answered Blacksnake. "Now, I pray you, go quickly and summon the snake doctor, for I am still very ill. The other day I came up here to get this fine nest of young woodpeckers, and was taken suddenly ill too ill, indeed, to move. You should have the birds if I could get out of the way (they are behind me). Find the snake doctor, and when he assists me to get away you can get at the birds, which I will willingly give you for your trouble. I have lost all taste for them, my one thought is to get home and see if my eggs are hatching. It is now time for that."

Greedy Owl cared nothing for Blacksnake's illness, but she was anxious to obtain possession of the young woodpeckers. She was thrown off her guard too by Blacksnake's ignorance of what had befallen the eggs; she therefore set out with all speed for the pond where the old snake doctor lived.

She found it a long way to the pond, but she reached it at last, told her errand, and, without waiting for the doctor to accompany her, started back. When about half way to the tree, whom should she meet but her husband, flying towards her in great agitation. She screamed with fright at sight of him, he with joy at sight of her.

"What has happened to the nest?" she shrieked.

"What has brought you back to life?" he cried.

When they came close to each other there was a strange tale to tell and to be heard. Blacksnake had gone to Father Owl and told him his wife was lying almost dead upon the river bank, and wished much to see him ere she let her life slip through her nose. Poor Father Owl was never a very wise bird; he was not a sorcerer. He knew none of his wife's tricks, so, as Blacksnake promised that she would look after the nest, he set out for the river, but having lost his way was nearing the pond instead.

Owl shrieked with fury and dismay. No shovel jammed into the fire could have stopped her voice that night, no matter how many people tried to put the spell of silence on her in that way. Well she knew she should find a ruined nest and no friend Blacksnake watching over it. No, no, she did not expect to see Blacksnake again, but neither did she expect to hear her call from a secret place beneath the desolated home.

"Another time, my wicked enemy, you would better cover up your tracks, unless you wish to prove that what one can do another can do, and the same measure can be used for berries or meal."

Source: Adapted from *Old Rabbit the Voodoo and Other Sorcerers,* Mary A. Owen (New York: G. P. Putnam's Sons, 1893), pp. 239–244.

The Son Who Sought His Fortune

The following tale shows the obvious influence of the European Märchen or "wonder tale" a complex and highly structured fictional narrative that is popularly known as the "fairy tale." However, this African American version of the common plot of the success of the younger sibling who goes to seek his fortune and through the aid of a supernatural helper wins a bride and achieves high social status appears abbreviated and fragmented in comparison to most European and European American variants of the type. Certain traditional features of the tale continue to be emphasized, however: the unjust treatment and low status of the protagonist and the power of the "man of mysteries" to overcome the obstacles that lie in the young man's path. Social inequities were all too familiar to the African American bearers of this oral tradition, and conjuring was often seen as a tool for survival (See "Running Hand"). Therefore, references to these two features that continued to have relevance to African American culture may have been retained while others that were less meaningful were eliminated over time.

There was a very old king had three sons. He seemed to be getting old and feeble, and he loved all his boys. They was the apple of his heart. He was undecided who shall be the king to succeed him. He said, "My dear boys, if you all do well I want you to promise me one thing. The one of you who goes out and prospers better I will proclaim the smartest one of you and make him the heir to my kingdom, and all of my territory."

One lad, the youngest lad, he went out and learned to be a very fine carpenter. And the next older he went out and learned to be an expert shoemaker. And the oldest one learned to be a very fine bricklayer. And after all of them had been away about three years from their father's house they come back. So the father wanted to know what each one of them had done.

The youngest one said he was a carpenter. He showed his father what he could do. His father said, "My dear son, you have done well."

So the second son showed what he had learned to do. So his father said to him too, "My dear son, you have done well."

Then, he calls his eldest son and asks him what he has done, and when he told him he said, "My dear son, you have done well."

When he had seen what they all did he said to them, "My dear sons, you all have did splendidly, but I am going to make the eldest son my heir

When he heard this, the youngest lad left and went through some strange foreign lands. He traveled and traveled. He went to a house, to a big fine house and asked them for something to eat that he was hungry. That was the king's palace, Etonia Palace. The princess she seen him out the window there; they kept the princess in a sort of confinement. They didn't wish her to see any men at all, didn't want her to keep company at all, no one of her choice. They wanted her to marry some nobility there, a very old man.

When she seen the young fellow she really loved him. She throwed a note down to the fellow, told him she'd like to speak to him in the garden that night. When they met that night, they sat down and talked and became very good friends. Then, she saw one of the guards coming and she told the young fellow to hurry and leave her, "Royal Guards coming. They will surely kill you if they catch you in here."

Soon after, the king seen her sighing one day and asked her what she was sighing for. King said he would give her anything she asked.

She said, "I wish you would help that poor man." He sent for the young fellow and gave him six pieces of silver, gave him a suit of clothes to put on him, and sent him on his way. And the young man went to a wise man, a man of mysteries, and told him. "I would like to marry the king's daughter."

He gave him six pieces of silver the king had give him, and the wise man told him, said, "I want you to go to the king's house six mornings. I want you to go to the king's house back to the window where you were when the princess first saw you and get her to ask her daddy to let you come for six mornings." Said, "When you go there they gonna speak evil of you, but don't pay no attention to them, always go with a smile." And she pled with her father and went on and he came there.

And the sixth day when the young fellow went there this mystery man he had a very dear friend who lived in the city what handled all kinds of clothes. He was a man of mysteries that he had all ways of living, great influence. He asked his friend to lend him a very fine suit of clothes and borrowed his horse. On the sixth day he sent the lad there to the king's palace and he said, "My dear lad, why you came here so much to do me honor?"

The lad said, "I love you, king, because you're a great and noble king."

One day the king was out hunting, fox hunting. Y'know they get very thirsty on that day. The lad got information where the king was and he got a pitcher of ice water. So the king got a sympathetic feeling for the lad that he told the lad that he'd give him anything he wanted. The lad told him he wanted to marry his daughter. So the king agreed, and the lad married his daughter and they lived happy from that day and forever.

Source: Adapted from, "The Son Who Sought His Fortune," Arthur Huff Fauset. "Negro Folk Tales from the South (Alabama, Mississippi, Louisiana)," *Journal of American Folklore* 40 (1927): 213–303, pp. 245–246.

The Seventh Son

The following tale shares several motifs with the European folktale "Hansel and Gretel." Two children are abandoned in the woods by parents who are unable to support them. One sibling cleverly devises ways for the abandoned children to find their way back home. Birds destroy the trail markers on the second attempt at losing the siblings in the wilderness. They have an encounter with an evil forest dweller whom they outwit and rob of a treasure. If, in fact, the tale was borrowed from European tradition, it was localized to African American social and cultural settings. Instead of bread crumbs, mush is used to mark the path home. The devil and his wife and a cabin in the woods are substituted for a witch and a gingerbread house, and ether acquired from a doctor is used to subdue the devil. Finally, the tale concludes with a moral lesson regarding the proper treatment of children.

An old man had seven sons. And he was an old woodchopper, and he came to the conclusion that he couldn't feed them. Early one night he laid in bed and told his wife, "We have too many children. We can't feed them all. Best thing we can do, I think, is we'll lose two of them in the morning."

So the youngest and the next they taken them two along. But the youngest heard what his father said, and he gets up that morning early and goes to the brook. He fills both of his pockets full of stones, also his brother's pocket. So their father called them and took them away with him. He was going to lose them. It was still dark out, and they dropped rocks all the time till daylight broke.

Daylight broke and the old man stopped. He started choppin' wood. Everywhere the old man took them they dropped rocks. He put them in certain place in the woods and told them to stay there till he returned. Finally dark caught them and no one had returned. So they started following the rocks. They made a trail right back home.

The mother said, "Well, we have much more mush than we can finish tonight, and if they was here there would be something to eat for them, and they could enjoy it." Just at that time the seventh son knocked on the door. He surprised his parents, and after they walked in the mother got the mush for them. They enjoyed it that night.

For a couple of days after that the old man didn't say nothing. He was just wondering what to do. So one morning he woke them all up all at once. They didn't know anything about what was going on. When they called them up the seventh son thought of mush from the night he had been left in the woods. So he fills all his pockets with mush and gets his brother to do the same. So every step they took they dropped mush. Daylight came.

Well, of course, after daylight the birds see it and pick it all up. So the father chopped wood for a long while, then he put his sons in a spot and told them to wait there till he returned. So the father went away and never came back.

When the boys looked for the mush they couldn't find it because the birds ate it all up. So the seventh son said, "Well, we're lost." So he climbed a tall pine and looked around. He said, "I'll look and see if there is any light. Way over yonder I see a light. We're gonna travel that way."

So he had seen a light over in the east. He always remembered where the east was. He knew all the directions, north, east, south. They traveled, traveled all through the night and sure enough they found that light.

So they found the light, and it was at the devil's house. The seventh son knocked on the do' and asked the lady who answered the door for a place to lodge.

The lady said, "This is the devil's house. The devil is away just now but he will soon be back. I would give you a place to lodge but the devil eats children."

So the seventh son said, "We might just as well get eaten up by your husband as to get eaten up by animals in the woods. We'll take a chance."

The devil's wife said, "Aw right, come on in." So she gave them a bed to themselves. Pretty soon the devil came in. He said, "Um-m-m-m-m, I smell fresh meat."

His wife said, "I don't know what it is unless it is them two sheep that you killed."

The devil said, "No, I smell sheep, but I smell fresher meat than them." He went on inside the house and rambled around until he found the seventh son and his brother. The devil said, "Um-m-m-m-m, I'm gonna have a lovely breakfast tomorrow." The devil had two daughters, and he took the two white caps from off their heads and put them on the two boys. Then, about two hours after he put the caps on the two boys' heads it was dark, and he felt in the room for the two boys caps. But the seventh son had reversed the caps and put them back on the daughters' heads. The devil felt the cap and drew his knife. He cut both his daughter's heads off. Then the devil went out of the room.

The seventh son said to his brother, "Now brother, we got to travel now." So they started away as fast as they could go. The old man devil finds his two daughters the next morning, and he is as mad as can be. He said to his wife, "Gimme my twelve-mile boots." He puts on the twelve mile boots, and he is able to take twelve miles at every step. The seventh son sees the devil coming.

He said to his brother, "Get up under this rock." The devil comes right to that rock and goes to sleep. So the seventh son waits till the devil is sound asleep, and then he puts on the devil's boots and goes back to the devil's wife.

He says to her, "The devil's in big trouble. It'll take all his money to get him out. He says to get it and send it back by me." So the devil's wife gets all his money and gives it to the seventh son.

He started back and on his way he met a doctor with all kinds of stuff. He said, "Doctor, got any ether?"

The doctor said, "Yes."

He said, "Give me one hundred dollars worth." So he took the ether and put it in the devil's nose. He knowed he had him then. He told his brother to come out from under the rock. All that day they traveled. They didn't know where they were going. They were trying to find some people.

Unbeknown to them they got to their home. Their mother was in slumber. She was asleep dreaming about her sons. The seventh son knocked on the door.

She said, "Who that?"

He said, "It's me, your seventh son."

She recognized her two boys and grabbed them she was so happy to see them again.

So the seventh son said, "I have a wealth for me and you." So he took his mother and carried, her away that night. Next day he showed her the money. He bought a home, and next month he made his mother go back and go get the rest of the brothers, and made them wealthy. But he drove his father away. He said, "You didn't love your children enough to work for them and keep them, but you took them out in the woods where the wild animals could eat them, and you left them there all by themselves. But we found a way to save ourselves, and I stayed away from home till I made my fortune, then I came home. Now we don't need you. Let all fathers be well aware how they treat their children."

Source: Adapted from "The Seventh Son," Arthur Huff Fauset. "Negro Folk Tales from the South (Alabama, Mississippi, Louisiana),." *Journal of American Folklore* 40 (1927): 213–303, pp. 255–257.

Mathew "Bones" Hooks, Cowboy

Despite his contributions, few contemporary Americans outside the occasional history buff know the particulars of the life of the African American cowboy. African American cowboys contended not only with the grueling labor and deprivation of their occupation, but as "Bones" Hooks's following personal experience narratives recount they contended with racism as well.

Mathew (Bones) Hooks, who for years worked on Panhandle ranches as a horse wrangler and "bronc-buster," knows many tales of cowboy life in the early days, but he refuses to tell the most interesting ones "because it would rattle skeletons in the closets of prominent families"—old-timers who are still living or their descendants.

Bones, without calling embarrassing names, recites a case in point. Called as a witness before a grand jury recently, he recognized in the judge a pioneer cattleman.

"Bones, do you know anyone who has stolen cattle"—the judge caught the glint of memory in the piercing black eyes and hastily added "now?" And Bones, whose lips had been forming the question, "What time are you talking about, Judge?" could honestly answer, "No."

Both of them were recalling a certain day in the past when the judge, then a young man just starting out in the cattle business, and a young Negro cowboy drove a fine young male calf from the pastures of the Capitol Syndicate (XIT Ranch) to the white man's ranch.

The embryo cattleman could not afford to buy a good bull—Bones said "surly;" he would not use the word "bull" before a lady interviewer—which he needed for breeding purposes. He went to the Negro cowboy, who was working on the XIT at the time, and asked him if he knew where he could get one. Bones looked over the range and, seeing no one near, selected a fine-looking calf, which they drove toward the home ranch of the judge-to-be. Coming upon a still better animal, Bones exchanged the tired calf for the other, and proceeded an his way.

The young rancher tied up the calf until it was weaned to keep it from getting back with the mother cow. "It took about four days to wean a calf," said Bones. "After that time he would go down to the water hole and drink and then mosey out on the range and eating grass and forget all about him mamma."

Bones, who was very young when he was working on Panhandle ranches in the days before law and order came, has good reason to remember the Vigilantes who took the place of the "law" in those days. The Negro cowboy, since the death of "Skillety Bill" Johnson of Canadian, is the last person to know the password of the Vigilantes.

When Skillety Bill died, persons interested in the history of the Panhandle went through his personal effects. Among his papers they found the notation that Bones was the only person left knowing the password. These same persons went to Bones and asked for the password, but he refused. "I am going to keep my word until I die," he said, "and then my papers will be left to the [museum?]. The password will be among them."

According to Bones, Skillety Bill got his name because he worked on the Frying Pan Ranch. Cowboys from the Panhandle ranches in the early days went to early Sweetwater, Texas, adjacent to Fort Elliott, to "celebrate." Negro women in the families of colored troops stationed at the army post would see Bill Johnson coming and say "There comes that Skillety (their version of Frying Pan) Bill fellow."

Skillety Bill figured in one of the most important episodes in Bones' life. The Negro boy was working at the time in old Greer County, which was a part of the "neutral Strip," locally called a second "No Man's Land." Bones, young and inexperienced, had hired out to wrangle horses for a certain cattleman.

One day, while be was tending the horses and minding his own business, Vigilantes rode up and asked him, "Are you working for those cattlemen down the creek?" Bones admitted that he was. Before he could say "Jack Robinson," the Vigilantes jerked him up and started to hang him on the nearest tree. They had already hanged the two white men mentioned to other convenient trees.

One of them Bones knew to be innocent. He was only a young boy who had come into the country looking for work two or three days before, who like himself, had hired out to the first men that offered him a job. But the Vigilantes, catching both of the white men with a herd of stolen cattle, took only circumstantial evidence into consideration and hanged them both.

Bones was certain that they were going to add him to their victims, when Skillety Bill spoke up in behalf of the colored lad, saying that he was a mere boy, wrangling horses for the boss and only carrying out orders of the cattle thief, whom he had taken to be a *bona fide* cattleman.

"A red-haired man astride a limb of the tree gave the rope around my neck a rough jerk," Bones vividly recalled; "and said, 'Aw, come on, let's got it over with;' but Skillety Bill saved my life."

After this narrow escape, Bones went into Oklahoma (then the Indian Territory) and so successfully "lost" himself that his own family and others thought him dead. At last he ventured back into Greer County. Walking through the streets of a Panhandle town, which he refuses to name, he came face to face with the sheriff (Skillety Bill).

The sheriff looked at him closely and finally said, "I thought you were dead. How long are you going to be here?"

"Only a little bit—a few days." Bones replied.

The sheriff started off down the street, turned back, and said, "How long did you say you were going to be in town? Did you say 'a little bit'?"

Bones, answered quickly, "Yes, sir, a little bit." He knew what would happen to him if he did not get out of town in a "little bit"—and he got.

The pioneer Negro bronco-buster knows cowboy life as few white persons now living. He was an interested listener around the campfires of nearly every ranch in the Panhandle. He heard many a lurid tale around a cow-chip blaze—words that can not be repeated in the hearing of ladies or in polite society. "Every horse, every man, bread and other articles of the camp, had a nickname, often unmentionable in mixed groups," he said.

Bones recalls an incident that occurred during a visit of Mrs. Charles Goodnight to a camp one day. One of the cowboys, who did not know of the lady's presence, said, "Bones, bring me up a horse."

"Which one?"

"That old...," the cowboy stopped suddenly and clapped his hand over his mouth, preventing the escape of the horse's unmentionable name when he saw Mrs. Goodnight standing there. "You know which one I want," he added significantly.

Bones honors and reveres the pioneer women of his beloved Panhandle, because they helped him as they helped so many others. When the cowboys tormented him—as they were always doing in some fashion—they took his part and made the white boys stop shooting blank cartridges at his feet or whatever they were doing to him at the moment.

It was one of those pioneer women who taught Bones not to "cuss." His favorite by word was "I' God"—a corruption of "by God." This pioneer mother came to him one day and said, "Bones, young Bob is taking up your speech and I don't want him to say 'I' God.' I can't keep his from saying it as long as he hears you, so I'm going to have to break you of the habit. If you'll quit, I'll buy you a Sunday suit."

Bones wanted that suit. When Bob repeated the byword, the Negro boy would say, "Bob, white boys can get suits any time, but this the only way that I can get one. You mustn't say 'I 'God,' or I won't get that suit."

Bones, who attends every celebration of old-timers, at one of these recent gatherings met the daughter of one of the pioneer families for whom he used to work—he frequently associated with the children of the early settlers, especially the boys. He reminded her of the time when she was a very young lady indeed. At that time she had never seen a colored person.

"Remember when you first saw me eating with the other cowboys?" he said. "You peeked out from behind your mother's skirt and said, 'Mamma, one of them didn't wash his face.'"

Bones said that he usually ate with the other cow hands. Once, when someone objected to the presence of the Negro boy at the same table, a pioneer housewife told the objector, "Everyone is treated alike at my table."

"In the early days," Bones said in answer to a question, "when a cowboy died on the trail, accidentally or otherwise, he was buried in a hole dug in the sod without loss of time and without much ceremony. The name of the dead man was sent to his family if anyone knew his real name or who his people were."

"Later, coffins were made of pine boards. Those who died were buried as soon as possible in those days, for obvious reasons. Relatives and friends sat up with the dead to keep the cats and dogs away.

"Services for the dead were held by a friend or someone who was qualified— later by traveling preachers. Towns were far apart, and preachers and doctors had to go miles and miles to serve these communities."

"Meetings—church services—were held in the homes of pioneers until churches were built," he concluded.

Source: Interview of Bones Hooks. American Life Histories: Manuscripts from the Federal Writers' Project, 1936–1940. Ms. Div., Lib. of Congress. *American Memory.* Lib. of Congress, Washington. July 12, 2008.

How the Little Boy Went to Heaven

This tale of a child's longing for his dead father contains a veiled criticism of antebellum society. The boy is pitied by birds who help him attain his goal of reaching a heaven that is firmly rooted in the Christian image of the afterlife. His original quest to see his father is diminished, however, when he becomes overwhelmed by the splendor of heaven. At last he realizes that even this splendor cannot replace his longing for his mother. The narrative recalls the real sorrow of enslaved families whose members could be sold or relocated at their owners' whims. The compassion of wild animals and angels contrasted to the system that forces Mama Carline to work in the fields all day and spin all night to be reunited with her child emphasizes the cruelty of the latter.

A little boy's father died and went to heaven. The little boy wanted to go to heaven too. He wandered around in the woods and wanted all the birds to take him to heaven, but the birds all laughed at the little boy. He kept on begging the birds to please take him to heaven.

At last the little red bird she took pity on the little boy. She said she would take him to heaven as high as she can go. She said, "I can't take him clean up to heaven, because I can't fly high enough."

The little boy thinks if the red bird gets started, he can beg her to keep on 'til she gets clean to heaven.

So the little boy he gets on the red bird's back, and little red bird flies very high, and the little boy feels happy. Presently the little red bird says she can't go no higher. The little boy he looks, and he looks, but he don't see no heaven. The little boy he begs, he cries and cries. He begs the little red bird to go higher, but the little red bird she says she can't go no higher, and she flies round and round.

Presently Sis Crow comes sailing along, and she hears a great fuss, and she asks little red bird, "What's the matter?" Little red bird tells Sis Crow how the little boy is crying for her to take him to heaven, and she begs Sis Crow to take him on.

Sis Crow says she take him far as she can go, but she can't take him clean to heaven. Little red bird says, Sis Crow might fall in with King Eagle, and King Eagle can take him to heaven.

Sis Crow she says, "Yes, King Eagle can take him to heaven, 'cause King Eagle is the only bird that can look in the face of the Lord without winking."

So the little boy gets on Sis Crow's back, and he feels very happy, 'cause he gets started again. Presently Sis Crow says she can't go no higher. The little boy he looks and looks, but he can't see no heaven. He cries and cries, and begs Sis Crow to go higher. But, Sis Crow she says she can't go no higher, and she sails round and round, while she watches out for King Eagle. Presently King Eagle comes sailing along, and he hears a mighty fuss up there, and he asks Sis Crow, "What the matter?"

Sis Crow she tell King Eagle how the little boy is crying 'cause he wants to go to heaven to see his daddy, and she begs King Eagle to take him to heaven.

King Eagle he says he take him, but he can't fetch him back. He tells the little boy he will take him to heaven, if he won't ask him to fetch him back.

Then the little boy he gets on King Eagle's back, and they go higher and higher, 'til they get in the glory of the Lord. Then the little boy has to shut his eyes, it shines so bright. But King Eagle never shuts his eyes at all, and he puts the little boy inside the pearly gates, and the little boy was very happy.

But after a little bit the little boy begins to grieve mighty for his mama. He cries and he cries, and when the Angel asks him what the matter, he begs him to take a message to his mama. He begs the Angel to tell his mama to spin him a cord long enough so he can tie it on the gatepost and come down to her.

So the Angel she came down to earth, and she takes the little boy's message to his mama, and when she enters the house, she fills it with a great white light. And the little boy's mama she says when the cotton done picked she surely will spin the cord for him, but his mama she say she will have to work in the field by day, and she can only spin by night, and she have no light.

And the Angel she feels so sorry for the little boy crying, she tells his mama she will stand in the door for a light to spin by.

So Mama Carline all that season she keeps her place in the field with the hands by day, and by night the people hear her spinning-wheel all night long, and a bright light in her cabin.

And all that season the people going along the big road, they hear her spinning-wheel going all night long, and see a bright light in her cabin, looks like her house on fire.

So Mama Carline she spins every night, long night after night by the light the Angel makes, 'til the Angel tells her the cord is long enough. Then the

Angel takes the cord up to the little boy, and he ties it to the gatepost, and slides down to his mama.

Source: Adapted from "How the Little Boy Went to Heaven," Emma M. Backus. "Folk-Tales from Georgia," *Journal of American Folklore* 13 (1900): 19–32, pp. 30–32.

The Water of Life

The "quest theme" built upon an account of young man going out to seek his fortune is a typical plot in European folktales. The following African American tale, with its royal characters and palaces, seems to owe much of its story line to the contact between European American and African American tradition bearers. Many crucial features of the tale, however, such as the enslavement of the populace by a princess who wields a large black whip and the hero's transformation into a black crow, suggest elements of the African American historical experience. As a result, this narrative represents an example of the adaptation of borrowed European to express African American social conflicts.

There was a young lad whose mother had died. Before she died she gave him a ring and told him to wear that ring. She told him don't take it off ever in your life. It was a very peculiar ring, strangest ring in the world.

After she died, he went out to seek his fortune. As he was on his journey he went into a strange country what he had never seen before in his travels. Tired and hungry he sat down to rest and fell to sleep. There was an old lady passing by going to the well to draw water. She was sighing, see, and the young man asked the old lady what was she sighing about.

She said it was because she have lost her son, see. She said, "I had a son like you, see, but he was taken away from me."

He wanted to soften the old lady's heart, so he agreed to go and live with her family and be her godson. One day as he was there some of the nobility people seen him there, see, and they was wondered about him. They asked him why he lived there, because it was a law in that country for every young man to be taken to the palace to serve the princess. She was the heir to the throne. But when the young men went to the palace to visit they mysteriously disappear. No one knows where they goes.

When the nobility came to the queen they told her of the very fine young fellow. They told the princess of the lad they seen, and she sent some soldiers down to take him back to dine with the princess. She sent her carriage to escort him to the palace. When he came to the palace, they escorted him through the palace and they sat him down in a very fine dining room. She ordered the royal servants to fix their dinner in her private dining room. And when they got done with their dining, she taken the young fellow, carried him with her through her garden.

When they came to the garden there was a tunnel going through. As they were passing through there, great, large black dogs came in there rushing at them. She went a-lashing them with her whip and cutting blood from them with each lash, and they retreated.

As she got out of that dungeon there was a river there. She got near to the large stream of water. She waved a magic wand, and a boat appeared from the bottom of the water. She got in the boat, commanded him to get in the boat, and the boat went through the water like a shot out of a gun. They got to the shore of an island, a small island. Beautiful flowers and all kinds of fruit on the island. They tied the boat to the shore; they both of them went passing through her flowers and fruit trees. Then the princess went away and told him to wait for her. She was gone so long and he was eating the fruit and looking at the beautiful flowers and he thought he'd go and see what was holding her so long.

He went up through the garden on the island until he found a building there. He creeped up to that beautiful building. It had marble floors and beautiful paintings and all like that, and he seen her standing on the upper floor beside a very beautiful statue. And she was whipping that statue with her large black whip. And every time she whipped that statue it seemed to bleed, and when she got done whipping she told the statue, "If you do what I tell you, I will stop beating you." Statue didn't say a word, just bled. Every time she whipped it, it bled. She got tired of whipping, but it still bled. When she stopped, he slipped out of the building to keep her from seeing him.

She came back and they got into the boat. They cleaved the waters without any oars. They got to the end of the boat ride and walked through a little tunnel. Then the great big dogs came again, and she beat them some more with her whip. They just bled; she knocked blood out of the dogs and they retreated running and howling.

Then she told the lad to give her the ring he wore on his finger, the one his mother gave him. As he gave her the ring, she waved her magic wand, and he turned into a black crow. He went fluttering, and she cut at him with a dagger, tried to cut his wings off.

The lad flew to his godmother's home. And she knowed that it was him. He went whining, and she could tell that the crow really was him. About thirty miles from there lived a man of mysteries, know all things, and she went and seen him.

She told him of the great grievance she had with the wicked princess who had come and stolen her only godson who could comfort her in her declining years. He said he would do all he could to help her. He gave her a little something in a bottle to sprinkle. He told her when that crow comes round again to sprinkle it on him.

She went home. When the crow came again, she sprinkled it on the crow, and there was the boy who came to live with her. And when he did that she gave him a bottle to put in his pocket to prevent him from turning back.

He went back to the princess and asked for the ring. She got very angry and tried to turn him back to a crow. But every time she tried he sprinkled that stuff over him, and she couldn't do nothing.

Then he went through the garden and the dungeon. The dogs got at him, and he sprinkled the bottle of magic water on the hounds and waved a magic wand and the dogs ran off. Then he went to the palace and sprinkled water on the statue. She turned to a lady. She was a princess. This other princess was very jealous of her because the king liked her best. All the people loved her. Then they went back to the dungeon and sprinkled on the dogs. They turned into fine young men.

With the good princess brought back, there was peace and prosperity in that kingdom, and the people lived happy then and forever.

Source: Adapted from "The Magic Water," Arthur Huff Fauset. "Negro Folk Tales from the South (Alabama, Mississippi, Louisiana)," *Journal of American Folklore* 40 (1927): 213–303, pp. 246–248.

John Divides the Crops

John in the following tale represents the African American hero in a more contemporary setting than Brother Rabbit, Lapin, or even Bill of "The Champion." John trades his labor for the use of fields controlled by a white landowner ("Old Boss," "Captain"); he pays Old Boss a share of the crops produced, thus the label, "sharecropper." At its worst this system in many ways perpetuated the old plantation system by binding indebted tenants to the fields they tended for the Captain. Like the African American protagonist of the "John and Master" cycle, the clever sharecropper is able to use his wits to get the better of a socially powerful and wealthy antagonist, but unlike Rabbit, John's actions are justified and free of malice. The behavior of this stock hero is justified by an inequitable social hierarchy based on race and historical circumstances.

John, he heard there was an Old Boss up the river had twenty good acres to let out to a reliable man, and he went up there and told him that he was as good a man as he could find to farm that land.

"You got credentials?" Boss ask him.

John say, "You mean something to tell how good I can work?"

"That's it," Boss tell him. "And I don't want no shiftless, stupid black man settin' on my place."

John show him the calluses on his hands, say, "Boss, these calluses is my credentials, and as to being stupid, anyone can tell you I'm sharp man to come and sharecrop for you."

"Well, now," the Boss say, "we goin' to give it a try." He takes John with him and they go down to the twenty acres. Now Old Boss can't think nothin' except cotton, and he tell John this way: "We got to speak of the arrangements. You ready?"

John say, "Yes, Captain, I'm ready."

Boss say, "John, the arrangements is that we go half and half. That suit you?"

"Yes, sure suits me," John say.

"The way it is," Boss say, "I get the tops and you get the bottoms."

John ponder on it a while.

Boss say, thinkin' about all that cotton, "What's the matter, John don't it suit you?"

John tell him, "Why, yes, sir, Captain, it suits me fine. We can shake hands on that."

They shake hands on it and Boss went on home.

John, he went to work on that land, plowed it all up and harried it. Then he plant. But he don't plant cotton like Boss has in his mind, he plant 'taters. And about the time the 'taters has good green vines on 'em, John stop by Boss's house, say, "Captain, the crop is growin' mighty fine. You want to see how it looks?"

Boss say, "Yes, I'm comin' to look. Been meanin' to get down there long before this." When he get there he see John workin' in that great big tater patch.

"Captain," John tell him, "count of you ask for the tops and you give the bottoms, you sure got you'self a mighty fine crop of greens. I'm goin' to bring them over in the wagon soon as I dig out the 'taters."

Boss, he got a real sad look on him. He say, "Well, John, you sure fixed me that time. But I got one thing to tell you. Next year you better look out. Because I'm goin' to take the bottoms and you can take the tops."

John shake his head up and down. "That's sure a fair arrangement," he say, "and I'm ready to shake hands on it."

So they shake hands 'bout the next year's crop, and Boss went home.

Well the next year John don't plant 'taters, he plant the field with oats

This time the Boss don't stay away so long, and on the way down he meets with John on the road.

John say, "Captain, you come just at the right time. I sure want you to look at the crop. It's comin' along just fine."

When they was gettin' close to the field, John tell him, "Guess this is goin' to make you feel pretty happy, Captain, 'cause you takes the bottoms and leaves me the tops."

"Yes, John, this year I take the bottoms, but what you goin' to do with the tops sure mystifies me plenty."

Then they come to the field and Old Boss just stand there lookin'.

That crop sure is pretty, ain't it?" John say. "Never did see a better lookin' field of oats long as I been farmin'. You goin' to get a sizable lot of stalks Captain. Reckon it goin' to make good straw to bed down the horses.

Boss shake his head, say, "John you outsmart me. You never said you was plantin' oats. But it goin' to be different next year. It goin' to be so different you ain't goin' to like it one bit. The way it goin' to be, is that I am goin' to take the tops and the bottoms and you get what is left. All you get is the middle. And if you ain't ready to shake on it right now you can pack up and get in your wagon and find yourself a home elsewhere."

John, he pondered some on that one.

"Well," Old Boss say, "what's it goin' to be?"

"It looks like they isn't too much in it for me," John say, "but you been good to me on this place, Captain, and I'm goin' to take that proposition and shake on it."

The next year John plowed up all his twenty acres and harried the ground good, and after that he planted his crop. Old Boss was pretty busy with things, but 'round the middle of July he considered he better go over and see how John's field is doin'. He met John on the road again.

John say, "Old Boss, I was just on the way to get you. It's a real nice crop I got and I want you to see it."

And when they got to John's field, what you think Old Boss found? All John had planted was corn, twenty acres of it.

"You sure got a mighty fine stand of tassels above and stalks at the bottom," John say. "But me and my family prefers the ears in the middle. What kind of arrangement you want to make for next year?"

Old Boss say, "John, next year they ain't goin' to be no top, bottom, or middle arrangement. I'll take same as you, just half and half."

Source: Adapted from "John Sharecrops for Old Boss," Harold Courlander. *A Treasury of Afro-American Folklore* (New York: Marlowe and Company, 1996 [1976]), pp. 438–440.

Railway Chefs

The Pullman Palace Car Company leased and staffed Pullman cars to the railroads. The Pullman Company was a major employer of African Americans from the mid-nineteenth century. An African American–led labor union, the Brotherhood of Sleeping Car Porters, was established in 1925 in an effort to improve working conditions for this predominantly black body of workers. The following personal experience tales illustrate the conditions that prevailed in the lives of these African American railway employees in the early twentieth century and the means they developed for coping with such conditions.

CHEF SAMPSON LANDS MR. TROUT

There were few refuges for African Americans from the realities of racial discrimination throughout much of the early twentieth century. Therefore, the following personal legend describing Chef Sampson's triumph over his white supervisor is particularly striking. Chief Sampson, like Rabbit in an earlier historical period, uses attitude, words, and wit against a stronger opponent.

When we were running on the Pennsy, there was an old chef on our run who was the most onery old cuss you ever heard of. His name was Sampson and he could out-cuss a blue streak. He was a dictator in his kitchen and there was the Devil to pay any time the dining car waiters and cooks' assistants did not toe the line as far as chef's kitchen rules were concerned.

There was one thing he was particularly mean about. He didn't allow anybody, not even the steward or second cook, to go into his ice box. The steward had the right to, of course, but even he used to humor the old man because he was so efficient in his work. And any time the second or third cooks wanted anything, they had to say: "Going in, Chef!" Meaning, of course, the ice box.

Well, if he felt in the mood, he'd say: "Go 'head in!"

If he didn't, the answer would be: "Wait a minute. I'll get it for you. I got my box arranged just like I want it and I don't want it mixed up."

We also had an inspector named Mister Trout. He was a tall, rangy, mean-looking white man from down in Georgia. He used to pop up unexpectedly in all sort of little out of the way stations, board the train and start prowling around, seeing what he sees.

Well, this day he climbs aboard at Altoona and just when we're speeding through the mountains to Pittsburgh, Old Man Trout eases back into the kitchen and starts rummaging through Chef's ice box. Chef had his back turned and was busy chopping some onions on a board near the window. He heard the commotion, however, and, without turning around said: "Get your nose outta that ice box."

Old Man Trout said nothing, but continued his inspection.

"Get outta that ice box, I say!" Chef repeated, still without turning around.

Old Man Trout straightened up to his full six, rawbony feet, took one contemptuous look at Chef Sampson and said: "Who do you think you're talkin' to? My name is TROUT!"

Chef Sampson stared back as cool as you please. Finally he drawled:

"I wouldn't give a hoot if it's CATFISH. You git duh hell outa my ice box!"

CHEF WATKINS' ALIBI

As this second story illustrates, not all railway chefs were of the same caliber. While Chef Sampson provided a model of strength and pride, Chef Watkins stands out as a an example of the ways in which power can corrupt. When Chef Watkins is humiliated, the storyteller and his audience alike take satisfaction in his downfall.

Chef Watkins was a short, fat squatty little man with the meanest disposition of any cook I've ever known; and I've known some mean ones in my time. He had a jet black skin and a belly on him that shook like tapioca when he was working the lunch-hour rush. He could cuss like a top-sergeant and seemed to take a fiendish delight in giving the boys who worked for him a hard time.

When we had taken about as much of his mistreatment as we could stand, the boys got together and hatched up a plot to get rid of him. The trouble was, he stood in too well with the big bosses. He was one of those kow-towing, old-fashioned, lackeys who would grin and yes a white man to death and give his own people misery from morning till night.

We all knew that Chef Watkins was killing the Company for everything he could steal. He had bought a huge, rambling old country house down in Maryland and a large breeding farm for jumping horses and prize stock... and you can't do that on what the Pullman Company pays you even if you have worked for them twenty years and have full seniority rating.

Nothing was too big or too small for him to steal. He had worked out a system with the commissary steward, and between them they did an awful lot of bill padding. In addition to that, he used to throw hams, chickens, legs of lamb and anything else off to his wife or children whenever he passed his place near Bowie. You know, that junction where the Pennsy crosses the Seaboard?

Well, the boys got together and decided that Old Cheffie had to go. So what we did was to drop a little hint here and there to Mr. Palmer, our chief steward, that if he'd just happen around the kitchen when we were nearing that Seaboard crossing, he might find out what was happening to all our missing supplies that he was catching hell about back in the Now York commissary.

To make it short and sweet, when we neared the junction this day, Chef Watkins was busy, as usual, getting his hams and chickens together to toss out the window to his wife who was armed, as was customary, with her old potato sack in which she carried home the bacon; not to mention eggs (well-packed of course).

Just as the train slowed down and the chef leaned back, ham poised like a football about to take flight, Old Man Palmer drawled in that deep Southern accent, as only Old Man Palmer could: "What do you think you're doin' there, Watkins?"

Well, you could have knocked the chef over with a feather. He stumbled, coughed and did everything but turn pale. It's the only time I've ever seen him stuck for words.

"Know one thing, Mr. Palmer?" he finally spluttered. "There's a ol' black, mean-mouthed woman who stands out there by the crossin' and cusses me an' calls me all sorta names ever time I pass here, an' it makes me so mad I grab up the first thing I get my hands on an throws it at her."

Source: Byrd, Frank. Interview of Leroy Spriggs, American Life Histories: Manuscripts from the Federal Writers' Project, 1936–1940. Ms. Div., Lib. of Congress. *American Memory.* Lib. of Congress, Washington. October 12, 2005. http://memory.loc.gov/ammem/wpaintro/wpahome.html

Brother Rabbit Gets Brother Bear Churched

Playing his familiar role of trickster hero, Brother Rabbit employs audacity as well as wit to escape his rightful punishment at the expense of his victim, Brother Bear. The deceit demonstrated by Rabbit in passing along one of his own crimes to Bear resembles the behavior of another stock character in African American folklore—the hypocritical preacher. Bear's punishment of being "churched" signifies a formal eviction from membership in his congregation. In the rural southern communities in which stories such as this arose, the church was a powerful force in social life. Rabbit as the hypocritical steward, who by the power of his office was able to make Bear an outcast, demonstrates the power of this social institution.

One year, Brother Bear he had a pen of fine hogs just ready for the smokehouse. But just before the Christmas season come on, every morning when Brother Bear fetched out his corn to feed the hogs, Brother Bear he done count them, and he find one gone, and the next morning Brother Bear done count them, and he find one more gone, and so it go until nigh about the last one of Brother Bear's fine fat hogs done gone.

Now Brother Bear he allowed that he was bound to find out who the thief that steal his hogs was, so all during the Christmas holidays Brother Bear he visited about among his neighbors constantly, and they all said, "What's come over Brother Bear that he's getting that sociable?"

But When Brother Bear was visiting, Brother Bear he be a-looking, and he be a-smelling for them fine hogs.

Well, Brother Bear he go to visit Brother Fox, and he don't see nothing and he don't smell nothing. Then Brother Bear he go to visit Sis Coon, but he don't smell nothing and he don't see nothing. Then Brother Bear he call on Brother Wolf, but he don't see nothing and he don't smell nothing.

Then Brother Bear he call on Brother Rabbit. Brother Bear he knock on the door, and Miss Rabbit she open the door, and invite Brother Bear in. Brother Bear he say, "Where's Brother Rabbit?"

Miss Rabbit she say, "Brother Rabbit's gone to quarterly meeting, being as he one of the stewards of the church." Miss Rabbit say, "Brother Rabbit just feel bound to attend quarterly meeting."

Brother Bear he say he wanted a fresh drink, and he go out to the well-house, and he see where they had been killing hogs. Now Brother Bear he knows Brother Rabbit didn't put no hogs up in the pen. Brother Bear he walk round and round, and he say, "I smell the blood of my land." And Brother Bear he fault Miss Rabbit with Brother Rabbit stealing all his fine hogs, and Brother Bear he say how he going straight up to quarterly meeting to church Brother Rabbit (and he a steward of the church). Brother Bear he roll his hands and arms in the blood and he say he going take the proof.

Now Miss Rabbit certainly is a faithful wife. When Brother Bear started off down the big road towards the quarterly meeting, Miss Rabbit she took a shortcut through the woods, lipity clipity. She got there before Brother Bear.

Miss Rabbit she went in and took a seat alongside Brother Rabbit. She whispered in his ear, "Trouble trouble, watch out. Brother Bear he said he smelled the blood of his land, trouble trouble."

Brother Rabbit he said, "Hush your mouth," and he go on with the meeting. Now Brother Bear ain't the onliest man that had been losing hogs that Christmas. Brother Wolf he done lost some of his fine shoats. Somebody done take his onliest hog out of Brother Fox pen. They take it up in meeting and make it subject of inquiry. They put the problem of solving the mystery on old Brother Rabbit, so the old man don't know which way he going to get to, when Brother Bear walk in, and his hands and arms covered with the blood, that he took to prove old Brother Rabbit was guilty before the whole meeting.

Directly Brother Bear walked in the door with the blood on his hands. Brother Rabbit he clapped his hands and he shouted, "Praise the Lord, brethren! The Lord done delivered me and brought forth his witness!" The people were all so distracted they don't listen to a word poor old Brother Bear say, but they all talk, and take votes, and they church old Brother Bear right there; and that why old Brother Bear ain't no churchman. But Brother Rabbit he run the church yet, and they say how he never misses quarterly meeting.

Source: Adapted from "When Brer Rabbit Get Brer Bear Churched," Emma M. Backus. "Folk-Tales from Georgia," *Journal of American Folklore* 13 (1900): 19–32, pp. 19–20.

Human Weakness

"Preacher" is a stock character in African American comic folktale (See also "Wait Til Emmet Comes"). As in the following narrative, the common thread holding Preacher tales together is the revelation that he shares all the weaknesses of his congregation. "Human Weakness" goes on to make light of the practice of confession that characterizes the Christian religions to which most Africans were converted upon arrival in the Americas.

There was a big camp meeting going on over at Selma (Alabama), one of the biggest they'd had for a long time. The preachers had come from all over, and they were spelling each other in the pulpit. First one would get up and give those people a sermon on Noah, then another would get up and preach on Jonah, and after him another one would preach on the Revelations of John the Revelator. The ones who weren't preaching at the moment sat behind and urged the preacher on. There was a lot of moaning, groaning, and jumping in the tent that day, and lots of folks being saved. After a while it got pretty hot, and the preachers gave a one-hour intermission so people could go get some lemonade and refresh themselves.

There were seven or eight preachers in the bunch, and they went next door, where they had pitched a small tent, and took off their coats and fanned themselves and had some lemonade. After they'd sat around a while, one of them said, "Brothers, we done a lot of talking this morning about the Good Book and human weakness. I got to say something on that. There ain't none of us is perfect in the sight of the Lord, and that includes us. I believe it would do us a powerful lot of good to humble ourselves and speak out on our own human weaknesses. Ain't that a fact?"

"Yes, Brother, it's the truth," the other preachers said, "ain't no one without a human weakness."

"Well, then," the first preacher said, "who want to begin?" Since no one else seemed ready to speak out on the subject of human weakness he said, "Looks like I am the one got to get the ball rolling. Brothers my human weakness is laziness. I can't tell you how lazy I get some times in doing the

Lord's work. I don't mind putting in a day, mind you, but I get downright sluggish on the overtime. I surely got to reform myself."

"That," said another preacher, "ain't nothing at all compared to my human weakness, which is liquid corn, moonshine. I just can't resist it. That's what my human weakness is all about, Brothers, and I'm a sorry man for it."

"Yes, that's bad, brother," another preacher said, "and I got something to match it. My weakness is gambling. That old Jack of Diamonds and Ace of Spades got me going. There ain't nothing makes me feel so good as playing cards at one dime a point. It sure gives me shame to say it, but all Satan got to do is flash a deck at me and I'm lost."

"Brothers," the next preacher said, "we're all in need of reform, but of all the human weaknesses I heard of in here today, mine is the weakest. My problem is women. I just can't keep my mind off any good looking gal, or any ugly gal neither. Seem like the Devil has got his hold on me for sure."

Every one of those preachers testified what was on his mind, all except one who never said a word. And at last the one who started the testifying in the first place said to him, "Well, Brother John, we heard from everybody except you. Ain't you going to join in?"

Brother John said, "Yes, I been thinking on it, but my weakness is a bad one."

"Ain't nothing too bad for the Lord to hear," the first one said. "Get on with it, Brother John."

Brother John said, "Brothers, my weakness ain't just bad, it's terrible."

"Tell it out," one of the preachers said, "it'll wash your soul clean."

"I sure hate to tell you," Brother John said, "but my human weak is gossip, and I can't hardly wait to get out of here."

Source: Adapted from "Human Weakness," Harold Courlander. *A Treasury of Afro-American Folklore* (New York: Marlowe and Company, 1996 [1976]), pp. 459–461.

Running Hand

The "hand" is actually an amulet or charm, often a bag filled with magical objects or substances. Despite the supernatural elements of the following brief tale, the major focus is on the resentment "John," the slave Everyman, holds toward his master and on the need to keep this resentment in check.

An old conjure man said he would give John a hand so he could sass his master, cuss him out. The conjure man said, "Put it in your pocket, keep your hand on it."

The master passed along; said, "John!"

John answered, "Who's that callin' me?"

Master said to the overseer, "Take him to the barn and give him around one hundred with the whip." The overseer whipped him, cut him all up, washed him down with salt an' water.

John went back and told the conjure man, "I went and sassed Master. Master like to tore me up."

Conjure man said," I give you a running hand. Why didn't you run?"

Source: Adapted from "Running Hand," Portia Smiley. "Folk-Lore from Virginia, South Carolina, Georgia, Alabama, and Florida," *Journal of American Folklore* 32 (1919): 357–383, p. 365.

The Irishmen and the Deer

In this pair of ethnic jokes, the Irishman is again cast as the numskull figure (see "The Irishmen and the Moon" for a similar characterization of the Irishman character). The comic twists of both of these narratives depends on an acceptance of the Irishman character as a "tenderfoot," uninitiated to life outside the city. Comic tales featuring the Irishman as an unsuccessful hunter were popular among African American audiences in the late nineteenth and early twentieth centuries

Some men went hunting, and they put an Irishman on the stand where the deer would pass, and went off in other directions. Pretty soon the deer passed directly by the stand, and the Irishman stood and looked at him.

The others came in at noon, and they all asked the Irishman why he did not shoot the deer when it passed so near. The Irishman said, "Why, it was no use; if he kept on as fast as he was going, he'd kill himself anyway."

Once upon a time some Irishmen went out deer-hunting. As a rule, a deer will have a certain path along which he will run whenever he is chased. The first time he is chased he generally gets by, because no one knows his path, but the next time someone is apt to be on the watch in that place. So it was with these men.

They made plans for the chase, which were as follows. The leader says to his friend, "Pat, youse get down yonder and sit by the road in some bushes. Don't holler, but keep right quiet and easy, and when the deer comes you shoot him in the shoulder, and, faith and by Jesus, we'll have him!" The leader went another way to hark the dogs on.

By and by the dogs began. "Ough! ough !"

Pat cries very softly, "Faith and by Jesus, he's comin'!" He looks very hard to see the deer, and soon it comes breaking through the woods into sight. Pat jumps up to shoot, but in a second he stops to talk again. "Oh," he says, "that's a man? Say, mister, where are you going?" The deer says nothing, but keeps on running. "Why, you seem to be in a hurry!"

No reply. "Are you running from the dogs?" No reply. "Well, if you have not time to talk, you had better hurry on ; the dogs are crowding you."

After the dogs had passed, the leader came up and said, "What is the matter with you, Pat ? Why didn't you shoot the deer?"

"I've not seen the deer," says Pat. "I saw a man go along here with a chair on his head, seeming to be afraid of the dogs."

"What did you say, Pat?" says the leader.

"I said, go on, old man, for the dogs are close behind."

"What a fool you are," says the leader; "you shall never hunt with us again."

Source: Adapted from "The Irishmen and the Deer," *Journal of American Folklore* 12(1899): 227–228.

THE SUPERNATURAL

Possessed of Two Spirits

"Possessed of Two Spirits" is a personal experience narrative told by Braziel Robinson that accounts for the storyteller's belief in the powers of conjuration (African American folk magic) possessed by "two-headed doctors" (a reference to their power to operate in both the natural and supernatural world). In fictional tales, Rabbit is often said to be a folk doctor of this sort (See, for example, "Brother Rabbit Brings Brother Fox Back from the Dead"). The present narrative contains references to both culturally specific beliefs (the power of graveyard dirt, sometimes called "goofer dust," to affect the living) and more universal folk beliefs (the powers of second sight conferred by being "born with the caul," a delivery in which the birth sac is draped over the newborn's face).

I am not a preacher, but a member of the church, but I can make a. few remarks in church, I have a seat in conference. I can see spirits, I have two spirits, one that prowls around, and one that stays in my body. The reason I have two spirits is because I was born with a double caul. People can see spirits if they are born with one caul, but nobody can have two spirits unless they are born with a double caul. Very few people have two spirits.

I was walking along and met a strange spirit, and then I heard a stick crack behind me and turned round and heard my prowling spirit tell the strange spirit it was me, not to bother me, and then the strange spirit went away and left me alone. My two spirits are good spirits and have power over evil spirits, and unless my mind is evil, can keep me from harm. If my mind is evil my two spirits try to win me. If I won't listen to them, then they leave me and make room for evil spirits. and then I'm lost forever. Mine have never left me, and they won't if I can help it, as I shall try to keep in the path.

Spirits are around about all the time, dogs and horses can see them as well as people, they don't walk on the ground, I see them all the time, but I never speak to one unless he speaks to me first. I just walk along as if I saw nothing; you must never speak first to a spirit. When he speaks to me and I speak back I always cross myself, and if it is a good spirit, it tells me something to help me. If it is a bad spirit, it disappears; it can't stand the cross. Sometimes two or more spirits are together, but they are either all good, or all bad spirits. They don't mix like people on earth, good and bad together.

Good spirits have more power than bad spirits, but they can't keep the evil spirits from doing us harm. We were all born to have trouble, and only God can protect us. Sometimes the good spirits let the evil spirits try to make you fall, but I won't listen to the evil spirits.

When a person sees a spirit, he can tell whether it is a good spirit or a bad spirit by the color. Good spirits are always white, and bad spirits are always black. When a person sees a bad spirit, it sometimes looks like a black man with no head, and then changes into a black cat, dog, or hog, or cow. Sometimes the cow has only one horn and it stands out between the eyes. I never saw them change into a black bird; a man told me he saw one in the shape of a black owl, but I have seen good spirits change into white doves, but never saw one in shape of a cat. I have seen them in the shape of men and children, some with wings and some without. Then I have seen them look like a mist or a small white cloud. When a person is sick and meets good. spirits near enough to feel the air from their bodies, or wings, he generally gets well. Anyone can feel a spirit passing by, though only a few can see it. I've seen a great many together at one time, but that was generally about dusk. I never saw them flying two or three along together. Good and bad spirits fly, but a bad spirit can't fly away up high in the air, he is obliged to stay close to the ground. If a person follows a bad spirit, it will lead him into all kinds of bad places, in ditches, briers. A bad spirit is obliged to stay in the body where it was born, all the time. If one has two spirits, the one outside wanders about; it is not always with you. If it is near and sees any danger, it comes and tells the spirit inside of you, so it can keep you from harm. Sometimes it can't, for the danger is greater than any spirit can ward off, then one's got to look higher for help.

I've heard spirits talk to themselves. They talk in a whisper like. Sometimes you can tell what they're saying, and sometimes you can't. I don't think the spirit in the body has to suffer for the sins of the body it is in, as it is always telling you to do right. I can't tell, some things are hidden from us.

People born with a caul generally live to be old. The caul is always buried in a graveyard. Children born with a caul talk sooner than other children, and have lot more sense.

I was conjured in May 1898, while hoeing cotton. I took off my shoes and hoed two rows, then I felt strange, my feet begun to swell, and then my legs, and then, I couldn't walk. I had to stop and go home. Just as I stepped in the house, I felt the terriblest pain in my joints. I sat down and thought, and then looked in my shoes. I found some yellow dirt and knew it was graveyard dirt, then I knew I was conjured. I then hunted about to find if there was any conjure in the house and found a bag under my door-step. I opened the bag and found some small roots about an inch long, some black hair, a piece of snake skin, and some graveyard dirt, dark-yellow, right off some coffin. I took the bag and dug a hole in the public road in front of my house, and buried it with the dirt out of my shoes, and throwed some red pepper all around the house. I didn't get any better, and went and saw a root doctor, who told me he could take off the conjure, he gave me a cup of tea to drink and boiled up something and put it in a jug to wash my feet and legs with, but it ain't done me much good. He ain't got enough power. I am going to see one in Augusta [Georgia], who has great power, and can tell me who conjured me. They say root doctors have power over spirits, who will tell them who does the conjuring; they generally use herbs gathered on the changes of the moon, and must be got at night. People get conjure from the root doctors and one root doctor often works against another. The one that has the most power does the work.

People get most conjured by giving them snake's heads, lizards, and scorpions, dried and beat up into powder and putting it in the food or water they drink, and then they get full of the varmints; I saw a root doctor cut out of a man's leg a lizard and a grasshopper, and then he got well. Some conjure ain't to kill, but to make a person sick or make him have pain, and then conjure is put on the ground in the path where the person to be conjured goes. It is put down on a young moon, a growing moon, so the conjure will rise up and grow, so the person stepping over it will get conjured. Sometimes they roll it up in a ball and tie it to a string and hang it from a limb, so the person to be conjured, coming by, touches the ball, and the work's done, and he gets conjured in the part that strikes the ball. The ball is small and tied by a thread so a person can't see it. There are many ways to conjure, I knew a man that was conjured by putting graveyard dirt under his house in small piles, and it almost killed him and his wife. The dirt made holes in the ground, for it will always go back as deep as you got it. It goes down to where it naturally belongs.

Only root doctors can get the graveyard dirt; they know what kind to get and when. The haunts [ghosts] won't let everybody get it. They must get it through some kind of spell, for the graveyard dirt works trouble 'til it gets back into the ground, and then wears off. It must get down to the same depth it was took from, that is as deep as the coffin lid was from the surface of the ground.

Source: Adapted from "Braziel Robinson Possessed of Two Spirits." Roland Steiner. *Journal of American Folklore* 13 (1900): 226–228.

Ridden by the Night Hag

The fear of the night hag (the witch who comes in the night) is a terror that crosses cultures and regional boundaries. The concept of the witch shedding his or her skin to commit evil deeds is found not only in African American folk traditions, but in African, European, and Native American belief systems as well. The following personal experience narrative contains features both of European and African-descended folk belief. The terminology of being ridden (attacked) by a "night hag" or simply "hagging" is derived largely from European folklore, while the belief that the witch sheds his or her skin (the "wet bedclothes" Grimes describes) has continental African precedents. Folklorist David Hufford describes the hag experience as being associated with four common symptoms: (1) awakening, (2) hearing or seeing something come into the room and approach the bed, (3) being pressed on the chest and strangled, and (4) the inability to move or cry out. The hag experience is represented visually in John Henry Fuseli's (1741–1825) painting "The Nightmare."

My owner had an old black female slave whom he called Frankee. I always believed her to be a witch: circumstances to prove this, I shall hereafter state. He also had at one time, a number of carpenters at work in his yard. One of them, a man about my size, and resembling me very much in his dress, being dressed in a blue roundabout jacket. He came into the yard to his work one morning, with an umbrella in his hand. This old woman saw him come in, and thinking it was me, or pretending so to do, was the cause of my receiving a severe whipping, in the following manner.

My master having mislaid his umbrella, had been looking for it for some time, and on enquiring of her about it, she told him that she saw me come into the yard with it in my hand. I was then in the yard; he called to me, and said, "Where have you been sir?"

I replied, "Only to work about the yard, sir."

He then asked me where I was all night with his umbrella. I told him I had not been out of the yard, nor had I seen his umbrella. He said I was a liar, and that I had taken his umbrella away, and was seen to return with it in my hand this morning when coming into the yard. I told him it was not so, and that I knew nothing about it. He immediately fell foul of me with a large stick, and beat me most unmercifully, until I really thought he would kill me. I begged of him to desist, as I was perfectly innocent. He, not believing me, still continued to beat me, until his strength was entirely exhausted.

Some time after this, my mistress found his umbrella where she had placed it herself, having removed it from the place where he had left it, and gave it to him, saying, "You have beat him for nothing; he was innocent of it."

I was afterwards informed by another servant, of the circumstance. I then went to my master, and told him that he had beaten me most unmercifully, for a crime I was not guilty of, all through the insinuation of that old woman.

He replied, "No, by Gad, I never hit you a blow amiss; if you did not deserve it now, you did some other time."

I told him she must have been drunk or she would not have told him such a story. He said that could not be, as she never was allowed to have any liquor by her. I told him to look in her chest, and convince himself. He then enquired of her if she had any rum.

She said, "No sir, I have not a drop."

I then told him that if he would look in her chest, he would find it. He accordingly went, and found it.

He then said to her, "Hey, you old hag I have caught you in a lie." On this same account she appeared to be determined to kill me, by some means or other.

I slept in the same room with her under the kitchen. My blankets were on the floor. She had a straw bed on a bedstead about four paces from mine. My master slept directly over my head. I was convinced that this creature was a witch and would turn herself into almost any different shape she chose.

I have at different times of the night felt a singular sensation, such as people generally call the night-mare: I would feel her coming towards me, and endeavoring to make a noise, which I could quite plainly at first; but the nearer she approached me the more faintly I would cry out. I called to her, "Aunt Frankee! Aunt Frankee!" as plain as I could, until she got upon me and began to exercise her enchantments on me. I was then entirely speechless, making a noise like one apparently choking, or strangling.

My master had often heard me make this noise in the night, and had called to me, to know what was the matter; but as long as she remained there I could not answer. She would then leave me and go to her own bed. After my master had called to her a number of times. "Frankee, Frankee," when she got to her own bed, she would answer, "Sair?"

"What ails Theo? (a name I went by there, cutting short the name Theodore)."

She answered, "Hag ride him, sair."

He then called to me, telling me to go to sleep."

I could then, after she had left me, speak myself, and also have use of my limbs. I got up, and went to her bed, but I could not find her. I found her bed clothes wet. I kept feeling for her, but could not find her. Her bed was tumbled from head to foot. I was then convinced she was a witch, and that she rode me. I then lay across the corner of her bed without any covering, because I thought she would not dare to ride me on her own bed, although she was a witch. I have often, at the time she started from her own bed, in some shape or other, felt a shock, and the nearer she advanced towards me, the more severe the shock would be.

The next morning my master asked me what was the matter of me last night. I told him that some old witch rode me, and that old witch, is no other than old Frankee. He cursed me and called me a damned fool, and told me that if he heard any more of it, he would whip me. I then knew he did not believe in witchcraft.

He said, "Why don't she ride me? I will give her a dollar. Ride me you old hag, and I will give you a dollar."

I told him she would not dare to ride him.

Source: Adapted from "Life of William Grimes, the Runaway Slave, Written by Himself" (New York: self-published by William Grimes, 1825), pp. 23–25.

The Hunter and the Little Red Man

There was extensive cross-cultural borrowing between Native Americans of the Prairie and Plains cultures and African Americans in Arkansas, Missouri, Kentucky, Virginia, and other states in the region that, prior to the European American migrations to the far west, was labeled the "Southwest." One area of particular interest is folk belief. The following African American tale, with its emphasis on the woodpecker as a source of supernatural power who becomes the guardian spirit of a hunter, is an obvious adaptation of a Native American tale.

One evening, late, as a hunter and his dog were walking slowly toward home, they saw before them, in the narrow path that wound through the underbrush, a very strange little red man. He seemed to be very feeble, very old, very lame. He told them, in faint accents, that he was far from home, weary almost unto death, and ready to perish from long fasting.

The hunter made answer, "If you can reach my lodge you will be welcome there. I have plenty of food, and a bed of soft furs for you, but it depends on you to get to them. As you see, I have no horse to place at your disposal."

The little man replied more cheerfully than he had before spoken that he could not walk, that was quite impossible, but, as he was so small, he thought the dog could carry him; adding that he saw marks on the dog which showed he had been used to carrying a pack strapped on his back.

"That is very true," said the hunter. "When me move our lodge this kind and faithful animal does have a pack strapped on his back. Also my children ride him as if he were a pony, but I will not call on him to carry other burdens unless he is willing. It is one thing to help the family of which he is a part, quite another to be burdened by a stranger that, too, when he is already weary."

Then said the little man, "All that is true and reasonable, I acknowledge that, but may I be allowed to speak with the dog myself?"

The hunter gave permission, so the little red man called the dog close to him, and pleaded very touchingly that he might not be left to die alone in the thicket of hunger and fatigue. "Take me," he begged, piteously, "to the hunter's lodge. I am not heavy when I am at my best, and now I scarce weigh more than a flake of wild cotton."

The dog was an uncommonly good-natured fellow, so, although weary and footsore himself, he was won to allowing the little old man to ride him to the village.

When they arrived, the little man, as he dismounted, whispered in the dog's ear, "You shall lose nothing by this."

"Oh, that is very well," answered the dog. "You are quite welcome to my assistance. I desire no present." With that he walked off to the other dogs, who received him with sniffs and yelps of derision.

"We met that old man out yonder, too," said they, "but we were not fools enough to become his servants. Oh no! Not we. We have enough to do to serve those who feed us."

This shocked the dog, but he was not more shocked than his master. The people of the village were all jeering at the hunter.

"Ah!" said they, "it was you, was it, to whom it was left to bring that wretched cripple among us ? We saw him, but he was no relation of ours, not even a friend of our friends. With game growing scarcer all the time, did you do well to bring him to eat your children's meat?"

This made the hunter feel bad, but he did not let his guest know it. He fed the little man, he gave him a place by the fire, and he gave him a bed of furs.

The next morning, early, the little man awakened his host and said, "Owing to your kindness I am quite well again. Now I must be gone. One last favor I ask, will you and your dog walk a short distance with me?"

To this the hunter agreed readily. He was glad that the guest of whom his friends had so low an opinion would soon be gone. He first set before him what food could be found, then called the dog. When the little old man had eaten, off the three of them went, he leading at a pace with which the hunter and the dog could scarcely keep up.

"Stop! Stop, Grandfather!" cried the hunter, after a little while. "I perceive that you are making a mistake. You are going the way whence we came yesterday. Let us retrace our steps, before we go farther out of your way."

"Come yet a few more steps this way," said the little old man.

So they went on again a long way. Once again the hunter called out "Stop! Stop, Grandfather! You are making labor for yourself. The place where we found you is not far from here."

"Come yet a few steps more," urged the little man.

So they went on again until they came to the place where they had met the evening previous. "Stop! stop! Grandfather," cried the hunter. "We are on the spot where we found you yesterday."

"That is true," said the little man. "It is where I meant to bring you. Now, we will stop and talk a little. You only of all your tribe and relationship have I found worthy of any friendship or consideration. I think better of your dog than I do of your chief or holy men. For this reason I mean to confer benefits on you two that they may not even dream of gaining. I will make of you whatsoever you choose; I will make of your dog whatsoever he may choose after you are done. You two only befriended me, you two only will I befriend."

So saying, he shot up before them exceedingly tall and terrible. Nevertheless, as they were not of the kind that quails, they looked on him undauntedly.

"Wish!" commanded he who had been the little man, impatiently.

"Oh, great chief, make me the greatest of hunters!" cried the hunter.

"You shall be not only the greatest slayer of beasts, but also the greatest slayer of men," was the answer. "So I say, so shall it be."

Then turned he who had been the little man to the dog. "What do you choose?" asked he. "Will you be the holy man yourself and turn out that old weed-eater who holds the place?"

This the dog did not care for. "I have been treated disrespectfully," said he, "by the other animals. Wolves have taunted me for carrying burdens, young dogs have scorned my slowness, beavers have told me my teeth were rotten as last year's briers. Make me strong enough to be terrible to them all."

"Will you be a mountain lion?" asked he who had been little red man. The dog joyfully answered he would like that above all things. "Then a lion you are. So I say it, so shall it be," said he who had been the little red man.

After this the man shrank to the size he had been when the hunter and the dog first saw him. Immediately he took affectionate leave of them and ordered them to go home and wait patiently for their heart's desire to come to them.

The hunter and the dog started home, but after taking a few steps they looked back. No little red man was in sight, but a great woodpecker rose from the grass and flew away.

"This is strange. Where has our friend gone?" began the hunter to his old dog, but he did not finish what he was going to say. He looked into the usually mild and friendly eyes of his companion, they were changed to great yellow moons; his stature also was greatly increased. Awestruck, the hunter shrank back: at the same moment, with a fierce and terrible cry, the mighty lion who was a dog no longer bounded into the thicket and never again was seen by his former master.

The hunter made haste homeward and reached his lodge before the village was astir. He laid down and pretended to sleep late. When he finally rose up, his friends told him his guest was gone, without leave-taking. "Worse than that," they added, "he has stolen your dog, the faithful friend of your children."

The hunter heard them gravely, he said nothing. He thought of his dog's wish and its fulfilment. He made ready his arrows, he tried his bow-cord, he had prepared for him a quiver of panther skin. When all was done, he started out to hunt, but before he went he said to the people, "Lend me many horses. Game is not scarce where I go. I intend to I take with as much as they can carry."

The people thought he was bewitched by the little red man, his relations were sorrowful, but he was so persuasive that he had his way with them. They went along with him and saw his wonderful success. After that, he always brought plenty for all when every one else failed.

When there was a war with enemies, he went to battle and all fell before him. When the old chief died he took his place and ruled many years. During all that time he kept secret the cause of his success, but when he was about to die he told his sons as a warning to them to invite good fortune home and not drive it to the lodge of others.

Source: Adapted from *Old Rabbit the Voodoo and Other Sorcerers*, Mary A. Owen (New York: G. P. Putnam's Sons, 1893), pp. 84–90.

The Friendly Demon

Like "The Water of Life," a tale collected from the same folk performer, "The Friendly Demon" is likely to be of European origin. Unlike the former tale, however, this narrative shows little adaptation to the African American context.

This man he lived in the valley, see, an old man, and he traveled around, see, doing cobbling, very peculiar man, very peculiar. People often came to him for advice.

In a nearby city lived a lad about eighteen years of age. He started out to make his fortune, and he met this man, an this man asked him where he's going. He said he's going out to make his fortune, on his life journey to make his fortune. The old man told the boy to follow him. This man picked up a very large stone and told the young fellow to pick a big stone up, too. So the young fellow he couldn't pick up nothing. So they carried that stone on with them.

They got very hungry, and the man he said something on the stone, waved a magic wand on the stone, and it became a loaf of bread. And he said, "Come on, sit down, and eat something." So when they got ready to leave, the boy he picked up a large stone; the man he didn't pick up none. They went to traveling through the desert all that night.

Next morning they awoke, and the man waved his hand and a great fine palace stood upon the hill. A princess came from the palace and made them welcome. The old man said, "I'm going to the palace. I don't want you to say a word when you get there." Then he waved his hand, and he said something and the wind taken them and dropped them on a lonely spot. There he waved his hand and a great big stone came wide open.

The old man gave the young fellow a little magic wand in his hand, and said, "When you get through that door, there is all beautiful flowers and all kind of fruit to eat." Told him don't speak a word. And the boy got in there, and traveled picking up flowers. He got the flowers and all the fruit he could hold. His arms was just full of fruit. And he brought them to the entrance, but then he spoke a word.

As he spoke a word wild beasts rushed at him. Then he waved up his magic wand which the man gave him to open the metal door, and the man was outside. He was angry with the boy for disobeying what he said. He decided to leave the boy at his own mercy.

As the boy was there a long time wondering what to do, a little man came up to him. He got scared at the bearded man.

The little man asked him, "Why? Don't be afraid of me, I'm the friend of all who carry the magic wand. I will carry you any place you want. I'm the demon, I will obey you." So the boy commanded him to take him away from that place. So he flew and flew and dropped him down alone in a desert. All by himself, no one there. He was worrying and worrying.

He got hungry. So the little of man came an' asked him what was the matter. He said, "I am hungry." And in a few minutes a big hotel was built and all the servants were there to serve him and honor him as a king.

The little man looked at him, said, "What else you want me to do?" He said, "I want a fine suit like a king." He got him a suit fine as a king's. After that he stayed there. He finally got tired of living as a prince, so he called the little man. He came there, greeted him. He said, "What do you want?"

The boy said, "I want you take away all this and give me a horse. I want to go out and make my fortune, I want to make my own living."

After he got his horse and went on his way, he passed through a city and he saw a beautiful queen there. He was looking at the queen. As he passed by looking at her a man said, "What are you looking at? Do you know it's against the law to look at the beautiful queen? If the king catches you looking he will kill you."

The boy found out that the king had sent out for all the wise ones in the world and announced that any man could make his daughter laugh he would consent for his daughter to be his wife. So he got to thinking and the old man came again, asked him, "What do you want?"

He said, "I want to make the princess laugh. First, you have to get me the finest suit that ever a prince wore, gold, diamonds, silver, and gold, and gold buttons. I want the finest horse that ever lived. I want footmen dressed in gold and silver. I want bags of gold, diamonds, jewelry of all descriptions." So he went to the queen with his line of soldiers and bodyguard, and on his white horse. He had one of the peculiarest walking sticks that ever was known. That walking stick could dance, sing, squeal like a pig.

It made the princess smile. So the king consented for him and her to be married. The king said, "Before you marry her I want you to build a palace for my daughter." The king gave him a place for the palace.

So the boy asked the little man. He built the finest palace the world ever known. He said to the man, "I want diamonds, an' silver, shiny gold, door knobs of gold, roof glistened with gold." Finer then the king's palace himself. Everyone thought it was magic. No one thought any one could build like that overnight. He and the princess went there to live and they lived happy hereafter.

Source: Adapted from "The Friendly Demon," Arthur Huff Fauset. "Negro Folk Tales from the South (Alabama, Mississippi, Louisiana)," *Journal of American Folklore* 40 (1927): 213–303, pp. 248–250.

Courted by the Devil

This tale of the vain young woman who vowed to marry only a suitor dressed in gold warns against the dangers of greed. By allowing herself to be tempted by a desire for wealth and luxury, she invites the Devil to her door. The plot of the supernatural lover (most often the Devil or an animal transformed into human shape) has been found in both the United States and the Caribbean. Usually the young woman is saved by her brother's ability to see through the false front of the false suitor as is the case in the following tale. A final riddle contest for the young woman's soul is found in both African American and European narratives of this type.

One time a lady said she was never going to marry a man unless he was dressed in gold. Her father had a party, and a man came dressed in gold. A servant came and said, "Somebody's at the gate."

The man's son ran out and led him to where the people were.

"Looks as if you were having some to-do here."

"Yes," said the man of the house, "you better go and take part in the dancing with them." The man's daughter took the man dressed in gold for her partner. A little boy about twelve noticed him, and said, "Sister, don't you notice his feet?"

"What's wrong? Why, no!"

"Why, sister, they ain't nothin' but nubs. Notice them when he gets to dancing. You ask him what's the matter with his feet."

Then the boy said to the man dressed gold, "Friend, what's the matter with your feet?"

He said, "I fell in the fire when I was a little fellow like you, and my feet got burned off." Now his hand was burned too. He said he fell in the soap-pot when he was a small boy.

The man in gold, fixed it with the girl's father to be married. That night said he must go home. He planned to carry that man's daughter back with him.

She said, "You let brother go with me. I'm going to a strange place. I would like to have some of my people going with me."

He let the little boy go, and they got up in his buggy and got ready to ride off.

The little boy says, "Sister, don't you notice how he done? When he got up in his buggy, he threw out an egg. He said, 'Hop and skip. Betty, go along.'" Betty (his horse that was pulling the buggy) just flew. He went until he came to where was a great big smoke.

The girl said, "Mister, what sort of a big smoke is that? I can't go through that smoke." "Oh, dat my hired hand's burning off new ground to plant my crops. I go and lay that smoke. I'll make it disappear."

"Sister, don't you take notice what he said. 'Hop, skip, Betty,' until we came to this smoke. He stop Betty, he lay this smoke. Are you willing to go back home with me, sister? That man ain't nothing in the world but the Devil."

Then the little brother threw out an egg, and said, "Wheel, Betty!" And Betty wheeled around in the direction of their home. "Betty, go along! Hop and skip!" And Betty flew back home to her father.

And behold! The next morning what should we see but the Devil coming. He went up to the gate of the girl's house.

He said:

Anybody here? Anybody here?
Named Mary Brown from General Cling's town.

Then the lady's brother ran and got an old witch woman who could answer that old Devil man's questions. If that of woman couldn't answer one of the questions, he'd have got that girl to take back to Hell with him.

The old witch said:

"Somebody here, Somebody here.
Name Mary Brown General Cling's town."

The Devil asked:

What is whiter,
What is whiter,
Than any sheep's down In General Cling's town?

The witch answered:

Snow is whiter,
Snow is whiter,
Than any sheep's down In General Cling's town.

He asked:

What is greener,
What is greener,
Than any wheat growed In General Cling's town?

She said:

Grass is greener,
Grass is greener,
Than any wheat growed In General Cling's town.

The Devil asked:

What is bluer,
What is bluer,
Than anything down In General Cling's town?

She answered:

The sky is bluer,
The sky is bluer,
Than anything down In General Cling's town.

He asked:

What is louder,
What is louder,
Than any horns down In General Cling town?

The witch answered:

Thunder is louder,
Thunder is louder,
Than any horns down In General Cling town.

Then the Devil got mad and said he won the girl's soul, anyway.

The old witch said, "If you want a soul, take this one!" Then she took the sole off her shoe and threw it at him. He jumped at it and took it down to Hell with him.

Source: Adapted from "The Devil Marriage," Elsie Clews Parsons. "Tales from Guilford County, North Carolina," *Journal of American Folklore* 30 (1917): 168–200, pp. 181–183.

Married to a Boar Hog

The historical record shows that, in the wake of the colonial Revolution against the British, "United Empire Loyalists" (Tories) emigrated to the British Caribbean from the Carolinas taking with them their household slaves. This immigration, as well as immigration from the Caribbean to the United States and ongoing trade between the United States and the Caribbean provides at least part of the explanation for the continuing similarities between the folktale repertoires of the Caribbean and the American South. As an example, the marriage between a young woman and a supernatural figure such as a demon or an animal (boar, snake, bull, among others) in human disguise is a tale type that is found in both the United States and the West Indies (See "Courted by the Devil"). The young woman's savior is most often her brother, and the boy is despised because of some physical affliction. In this tale he has leprosy, in others the affliction is yaws, a club-foot, or an infestation of vermin. The physical ailment makes him despised, yet he is an "ol' witch boy" who is able to perceive the suitor's disguise and compel him to reveal himself. Commentators are in general agreement that this tale is of African origin.

There was a woman who had one daughter and one son. This boy was a coco-bay (leprosy) boy, and he was an old witch, too. This woman wouldn't allow the girl to court anybody, you know. So one day Brother Boar-Hog came there, properly dressed the same as any gentleman. When he wanted to drop off his clothes and turn back to his boar hog shape, he had a song to sing to make him change.

The day when this Brother Boar-Hog come to see the daughter, the son told his mother, "Ma, don't let sister marry to this man, for he's a boar-hog!" The mother drove him off, and said that he was rude. She said that this man was a gentleman.

He told the mother, "All right! You will see." One day the mother gave him some food to carry to this man, all tied up nicely on a tray. When the boy reach to the yard of the house he lived, he got behind a tree. While he got behind the tree, he saw this boar-hog rooting up the ground. And this boar-hog rooted all the ground, like ten men with forks. This boy stay behind the tree and saw all he did. When the boy saw him, he waited a little; then the boy said, "Ahem!"

Boar-Hog jumped around; he started to sing,—

> Indiana, Indiana, um, um!
> Indiana, Indiana, um, um!
> Indiana, Indiana, um, um!

That caused his clothes to jump right on him according as he sang the song. He stepped out, put his two hands in his pocket, and say, "Boy, see how I plough up this land!" He boasted about the work he did on the field. Then he said to the boy, "How long you been here?"

Boy said, "Just came." He took the food and carried it in the house, and told the boy all right, he can go home. The boy didn't go home. He got behind the tree again. When Brother Boar-Hog thought the boy was gone, he had a long trough, and he dumped all the food in the trough. He threw a bucket of water in too. Then, when he was done, he started to sing,

> Indiana, Indiana, um, um!
> Indiana, Indiana, um, um!
> Indiana, Indiana, um, um!

And all his clothes dropped off. He stuck his snout in the trough and ate the food. All that time the boy was watching him, you know.

The boy started for home now, and when he got there he told his mother all what he saw. His grandfather told him all right, they'll catch him. They'll catch Brother Boar Hog. The daughter an' mother didn't believe the boy, but the grandfather believed.

So that same afternoon this Brother Boar-Hog came to the house all dressed up in a frock-coat. As he came in the house, he started talking and laughing with the mother and daughter. During this time the old man had his gun prepared. Little boy took up his fife and started to play the same song he heard Brother Boar Hog sing:

> Indiana, Indiana, um, um!
> Indiana, Indiana, um, um!
> Indiana, Indiana, um, um!

Brother Boar-Hog said, "What a vulgar song that boy is singing!" He started to moving. He was not able to keep still, because his tail was coming out fast. Quick he said, "Stop it, stop it! Let's go out for a walk! Let's go out for a walk! I can't stay here."

So they all went out, the daughter, the mother, and the grandfather. After they was going on, they was talking when Brother Boar-Hog looked back, he saw the boy was coming. He said, "Where's that boy going, where's he going? Turn him back. I don't want to be in his company." So the grandfather told him to let the boy alone; let him go for a walk too. Grandfather said, "Play, boy! Play, boy!" The boy started:

> Indiana, Indiana, um, um!
> Indiana, Indiana, um, um!
> Indiana, Indiana, um, um!

Brother Boar Hog's beaver [hat] dropped off. Then he played on again the same song: his coat dropped, his shirt dropped. All dropped except his pants.

The old man told him, "Play, boy! Play, play, play!" And his pants dropped off. They saw Brother Boar Hog's long tail show, and he started to run. The old man pointed the gun at him and shot him dead.

> And I went through Miss Havercomb alley
> And I see a lead was bending;
> So the lead ben',
> So the story en'.

Source: Adapted from "The Chosen Suitor," John H. Johnson. "Folk-Lore from Antigua, British West Indies," *Journal of American Folklore* 34 (1921): 40–88, pp. 62–63.

Wait Til Emmet Comes

"Preacher" appears as an important stock character in African American comic tales such as the following. In many instances, Preacher is a hypo-critical con man who exploits his congregation for economic or social gain. In those cases, a trickster uses superior cunning to expose the sham holy man's schemes. In this narrative, no doubts are cast on Preacher's sincerity. Instead, when confronted by intensifying threats from the supernatural realm, he seems to turn from a philosophy embodied in his repeated phrase, "The Lord will surely take care of me," to an attitude framed by the proverb, "The Lord helps those who help themselves."

Once upon a time there was an old preacher who was riding to a church he served at some distance from his home when night overtook him and he got lost. As it grew darker and darker, he began to be afraid, but he bolstered up his courage by saying every little while, "The Lord will surely take care of me."

By and by he saw a light, and riding up to it, he discovered that it came from a cabin. Getting off his horse and tying it to a fence stake, he knocked at the cabin door. When the owner opened it, the old preacher told his trouble and asked to stay all night.

The man who answered the door replied, "Well, Parson, I certainly would like to keep you all night, but my cabin ain't got but one room in it and I got a wife and ten children. There just ain't no place for you to stay."

The old preacher leaned up against the side of the house and in a woebe-gone voice said, "Well, I guess the Lord will surely take care of me."

Then slowly untying his horse and getting on him, he started to ride on.

But the owner of the cabin stopped him and said, "Parson, you might sleep in the big house over there. There ain't nobody up there and the door ain't locked. You can put your horse in the barn and give him some hay and then you can walk right in. You'll find a big fireplace in the big room and the wood all laid for the fire. You can just touch a match to it and make yourself comfortable."

As the old preacher began to disappear into the dark, the other called out, "But, Parson, I didn't tell you that the house is haunted."

The old man hesitated for a moment, but finally rode away, saying, "Well, I guess the Lord surely will take care of me."

When he arrived at the place, he put his horse in the barn and gave him some hay. Then he moved over to the house, and sure enough, he found it unlocked. In the big room he found a great fireplace with an immense amount of wood all laid ready to kindle. He touched a match to it and in a few minutes had a big roaring fire. He lighted an oil lamp that was on a table and drawing up a big easy chair, he sat down and began to read his Bible. By and by the fire burnt down, leaving a great heap of red-hot coals.

The old man continued to read his Bible until he was aroused by a sudden noise in one corner of the room. Looking up, he saw a big cat, and it was a black cat, too. Slowly stretching himself, the cat walked over to the fire and flung himself into the bed of red-hot coals. Tossing them up with his feet, he rolled over in them, then shaking the ashes off himself, he walked over to the old man and sat down to one side of him, near his feet, looked up at him with his fiery-green eyes, licked out his long, red tongue, lashed his tail, and said, "Wait till Emmett comes."

The old man kept on reading his Bible, when all at once he heard a noise in another corner of the room, and looking up, he saw another black cat, big as a dog. Slowly stretching himself, he walked over to the bed of coals, threw himself into them, tumbled all around, and tossed them with his feet. Then he got up, shook the ashes off himself, walked over to the old man, and sat down near his feet on the opposite side from the first cat. He looked up at him with his fiery-green eyes, licked out his long, red tongue, lashed his tail, and asked the first cat, "Now what shall we do with him?"

The old man kept on reading his Bible and in a little while he heard a noise in a third corner of the room, and looking up, he saw a cat black as night and as big as a calf. He, too, got up, stretched himself, walked over to the bed of coals, and threw himself into them. He rolled over and over in them, tossed them with his feet, took some into his mouth, chewed them up and spat them out again. Then shaking the ashes off himself, he walked over to the old colored man and sat down right in front of him. He looked up at him with his fiery-green eyes, licked out his long, red tongue, lashed his tail, and said to the other cats, "Now what shall we do with him?"

They both answered, "Wait till Emmett comes."

The old preacher looked furtively around, slowly folded up his Bible, put it into his pocket, and said, "Well, gentlemen, I certainly am glad to have met up with you this evening, and I surely do admire for to have your company, but when Emmett comes, you tell him I done been here and have done went."

Source: Adapted from "Wait Til Emmet Comes," John Harrington Cox. "Negro Tales from West Virginia," *Journal of American Folklore* 47 (1934): 341–357, pp. 352–354.

Jean Lavallette and the Curse of the *Homme Rouge*

Supernatural vengeance against violators of the natural or social order is a universal theme in the world's folktales. Within the general narrative category, the legend of Jean Lavallette reveals the influence of cultural contact between African Americans and Native Americans inhabiting the Prairie and Plains culture areas of North America in the states of Arkansas, Missouri, Kentucky, Virginia. The belief in sorcerers with the ability to transform themselves into animal shapes is shared by both donor cultures, but the particular species featured in this tale, the woodpecker, shows a Native American rather than an African American emphasis (See also, "The Hunter and the Little Red Man"). Among other motifs particular to African American tradition is the belief in the malevolent black dogs alluded to as the companions of witches. The legend of Jean Lavallette is set in the midst of a larger storytelling context, a literary device employed by other collectors of African American folktales such as Joel Chandler Harris (the Uncle Remus books) and Zora Neale Hurston (Men and Mules). For additional background on the storyteller, "Big Angy," see "Red Feather."

"It," drawled Angy, "was Jean Lavallette that lived in the big plastered house in the upper bottom. Jean, he was rich. His papa gave him lots of land, lots of money."

"That was good," commented Granny, removing her pipe from her lips for a moment and stirring in the smoking bowl of it with her little finger; "but that is all there was good 'bout Jean, surely. I knowed him. In the points of fact I laid that poor, miserable sinner out. He was the leastest pretty corpse that ever fill up a coffin, that I know."

Angy cared nothing about Jean's lack of beauty as a corpse. She went right on with her story and stated, presumably to the back log of the fireplace, for her gaze never turned from it, that Jean was rich, that he married a beautiful wife, rich also in ponies, cattle, and land. So well off was he that he had no need to work. He became a very idle fellow, he laid on the grass and thought of nothing. Because one cannot always do nothing at all but eat and smoke, in mere wantonness of spirit he took to throwing stones at the birds. He began with the jays and robins, because they hopped about him and seemed to mock his laziness. When he had grown so expert at his wicked pastime of striking the little creatures that his very first throw stunned the one he aimed at, he was no more content to kill robins and jays, he slaughtered indiscriminately. Soon none were left but woodpeckers.

"Have care," said his friends to the bold fellow; "it is the worst of luck to get the ill-will of *le nain rouge* (the red dwarf). Some of these woodpeckers about here are real birds, but we know not which feathered skin hides the sorcerer or his children."

At such warnings Jean only laughed, or if he said anything it was to boast loudly that he had killed woodpeckers and would do it again.

Mark the result. After killing woodpeckers it was no time at all until he took to drink. Oh! Not merely to getting drunk at the dances and on holidays, that, to be sure, was to be expected, but he took to keeping the jug always at his right hand, and truly the weeds never had a chance to grow while it was still. Drink, drink, drink he would, from sunup to sundown, and from starlight to sunup again, even reaching out for the *eau-de-vie* (water of life) in his sleep. For the matter of that, he was never quite awake, nor quite asleep, though almost all the time he breathed as if the black dog of the witches were in his throat.

All things went wrong with the farm, in spite of Isabel's hard work and care, and because of this, the bewitched creature would sometimes rouse up and curse her. One day, when she was at work in the field, the baby took a fit and died, with Jean looking on and doing nothing. Isabel buried the baby and went home to her father.

Then the stock was stolen, the prairie-fire took the fences, the fodder rotted in the fields. He looked about him, one morning, frosty enough to brighten his wits, and found not even the smallest of small pigs was left to him. He was hungry, he went to catch a fish. As he started, he saw a woodpecker running along a tree-trunk. Full of fury, he swore terribly, and flung the empty whiskey jug directly at it.

In an instant, what a change ! The bird was a man, small, fierce, terrible, breathing flame. It flung a dart of lightning through him; it spit flames, into his eyes! He fell insensible from pain and fright, and knew no more until evening, when some neighbors happened to pass along, and found him more dead than alive. For a long time after they had restored his consciousness, he shrieked and raved of the little red man, and many times told all that had happened. Nothing, not even holy water, did him any good.

After much suffering he died, and no wonder, for there is no limit to the power of an offended *homme rouge* (red man).

Source: Adapted from *Old Rabbit the Voodoo and Other Sorcerers*, Mary A. Owen (New York: G. P. Putnam's Sons, 1893), pp. 75–77.

The Devil's Bride Escapes

The plot built around a vain young woman's marriage to a supernatural suitor recurs frequently in African American folklore (see also "Courted by the Devil" and "Married to a Boar Hog" for similar narratives). The following example, however, combines two internationally distributed subplots with the theme of the supernatural husband: the Bluebeard or Robber Bridegroom motif (husband as serial spouse murderer) and the Magical Flight (a chase is delayed by the transformation of a number of ordinary objects into obstacles that slow down a pursuer).

One day there was a pretty young girl, but she was very proud, and every time the young men came to court her, she found a pretext to send them away. One was too small, another was too tall, another had red hair; in short, she refused all her suitors. One day her mother said to her, "My daughter, you see that tall, tall tree in the middle of the river? I am going to put this pumpkin on the smallest branch at the top of the tree, and that young man who will be able to climb up and catch the pumpkin will be your husband."

The daughter said she had no objection, so they put a notice in the newspapers. The next week a crowd of young men presented themselves, and among them one who was beautifully dressed and exceedingly handsome. He was the Devil, but nobody knew him. The young girl told her mother: "I wish he would catch the pumpkin."

All the young men climbed on the tree, but no one could succeed in reaching the pumpkin. When the turn of the Devil came, in one minute he was up the tree, and had the pumpkin in his hand. As soon as he was down he said to the young girl: "Come now, come with me to my house."

The girl put on her best dress and went away with the Devil. On the road they met a man, who said to the Devil, "Give me my cravat and my collar which I had lent to you."

The Devil took off his cravat and his collar, and said, "Here, take your old cravat and your old collar."

A little further on, another man saw the Devil and told him: "Give me my shirt which I had lent you."

The Devil took off his shirt and said, "Here, here, take your old shirt."

A little further, he saw another man, who said to him, "Give me my cloak which I had lent to you."

The Devil took off his cloak, and said, "Here, here, take your old cloak."

A little further, another man asked for his trousers, then another one for his hat.

The Devil took off the trousers and the hat, and said, "Here, here, take your old trousers and your old hat." He came down from his carriage and disappeared for a few minutes, then he returned as well dressed as before.

The young lady was beginning to be very much frightened when they met another man, who said: "Give me my horses which I had lent to you."

The Devil gave him his four horses, and said to his wife, "Get down from the carriage and hitch yourself to it." She drew the carriage as far as the Devil's house, and was so frightened that her heart was almost in her mouth.

The Devil entered his garden, and said to his wife, "Remain here with my mother." As soon as he was gone the mother said to the young lady, "Ah! my daughter, you have taken a bad husband; you have married the Devil."

The poor girl was so sorry that she did not know what to do, and she said to the old woman: "Can you not tell me how I can run away?"

The old woman replied: "Yes, wait until tomorrow morning; but come, let me show you something." She opened the door of a little room, and said : "Look, my daughter." The girl looked in the room, and what did she see? A number of women hanging from a nail. She was so frightened that she asked the old woman if she could not hide her somewhere until the next morning. The woman said: "Yes, but let me tell you how you can escape from here. When the Devil tells you to give one sack of corn to his rooster which wakes him up in the morning, you will give him three sacks that he may eat more and not crow so early. Then you will go to the chicken house and take six dirty eggs. Take care not to take clean eggs; that will bring you bad luck."

The next morning the young lady gave the rooster three sacks of corn, she took her eggs, and ran away. When the rooster had finished eating his three sacks, he crowed, "Mr. Devil, awake quickly; some one has run away from the house!"

The Devil got up quickly and started running after his wife. The poor girl looked behind her, and saw smoke and fire—indeed, the Devil himself. She took an egg and broke it; a high wooden fence arose in the middle of the road. The Devil had to return home to get his golden axe to cut down the fence. After he had broken down the fence he took his axe to his house.

The girl looked behind her; she saw smoke and fire—the Devil himself. She broke another egg: there grew up an iron fence. The Devil went home to get his golden axe, and had to take it back after breaking the fence.

The girl looked again; there was fire and smoke. She broke another egg: a great fire rose up in the road. The Devil went to get his jar of water to put out the fire and then had to take the jar back.

The girl heard again a noise; it was fire and smoke. She broke another egg: a brick wall grew up. The Devil went to get his golden axe, and carried it back after breaking the wall.

The girl looked again; she saw fire and smoke. She broke another egg: a small river appeared, in which was a small canoe. She entered the canoe and crossed the river. The Devil was obliged to swim across.

The girl looked again; she saw fire and smoke. She broke another egg: a large river appeared. There was a big crocodile on the other side of the river warming himself in the sun. The girl sang: Grandmother, I pray you, cross me over; grandmother, I pray you, save my life. The crocodile said: "Climb on my back, my little one, I shall save your life."

The Devil saw in what way the girl had crossed the river, so he said to the crocodile, "Cross me over, crocodile; cross me over."

The crocodile replied: "Climb on my back; I shall cross you over." When he reached the middle of the river, he dived under the water, and the Devil was drowned.

When the girl had left her mother's house with her husband, her mother had said to her: "Well, my child, what do you wish me to do with your old white horse?"

The girl said to her mother: "I don't care what you do; put him out in the pasture and let him die if he wants to." However, when she crossed the river on the crocodile's back, she saw her old horse in the pasture, and she said to him, "I pray you, old body, save my life."

The horse replied, "Ah, you want me now to save your life; did you not tell your mother to let me die, if I wanted? Well, climb on my back, I shall carry you to your mother."

The girl soon reached her mother's house. She got down from the horse and kissed him, then she kissed her mother. She remained at home after that, and did not wish to marry again, after having had the Devil for her husband.

Source: Adapted from "The Devil's Marriage," Alcée Fortier. *Louisiana Folk-Tales* (Boston & New York, American Folk-Lore Society, 1895), pp. 69–75.

Aunt Harriet

*The following anecdotes of Aunt Harriet's conjuration were collected
and retold by Charles W. Chesnutt (1858–1932), an African American
author noted for fiction that addressed controversial racial themes.
The tale of "The Stolen Voice," also collected by Chesnutt, deals with
a similar case.*

Old Aunt Harriet—last name uncertain, since she had borne those of her
master, her mother, her putative father, and half a dozen husbands in
succession, no one of which seemed to take undisputed precedence—related
some very remarkable experiences. She at first manifested some reluctance
to speak of conjuration, in the lore of which she was said to be well versed;
but by listening patiently to her religious experiences—she was a dreamer of
dreams and a seer of visions—I was able now and then to draw a little upon
her reserves of superstition, if indeed her religion itself was much more than
superstition.

"Wen I wuz a gal 'bout eighteen or nineteen," she confided, "de w'ite folks
use' ter sen' me ter town ter fetch vegetables. One day I met a' ole conjuh man
name' Jerry Macdonal, an' he said some rough, ugly things ter me. I says, says
I, 'You mus' be a fool.' He didn' say nothin', but jes' looked at me wid 'is evil
eye. Wen I come 'long back, dat ole man wuz stan'in' in de road in front er his
house, an' w'en he seed me he stoop' down an' tech' de groun', jes' lack he
wuz pickin' up somethin', an' den went 'long back in 'is ya'd. De ve'y minute
I step' on de spot he tech', I felt a sha'p pain shoot thoo my right foot, it tu'n't
under me, an' I fell down in de road. I pick' myself up an' by de time I got
home, my foot wuz swoll' up twice its nachul size. I cried an' cried an' went
on, fer I knowed I'd be'n trick' by dat ole man. Dat night in my sleep a voice
spoke ter me an' says: 'Go an' git a plug er terbacker. Steep it in a skillet er
wa'm water. Strip it lengthways, an' bin' it ter de bottom er yo' foot'. 'I never
didn' use terbacker, an' I laid dere, an' says ter myse'f, 'My Lawd, wa't is dat,
wa't is dat!' Soon ez my foot got kind er easy, dat voice up an' speaks ag'in:
'Go an' git a plug er terbacker. Steep it in a skillet er wa'm water, an' bin' it
ter de bottom er yo' foot.' I scramble' ter my feet, got de money out er my
pocket, woke up de two little boys sleepin' on de flo', an' tol' 'em ter go ter

de sto' an' git me a plug er terbacker. Dey didn' want ter go, said de sto' wuz shet, an' de sto' keeper gone ter bed. But I chased 'em fo'th, an' dey found' de sto' keeper an' fetch' de terbacker—dey sho' did. I soaked it in de skillet, an' stripped it 'long by degrees, till I got ter de en', w'en I boun' it under my foot an' roun' my ankle. Den I kneel' down an' prayed, an' next mawnin de swellin' wuz all gone! Dat voice wus de Spirit er de Lawd talkin' ter me, it sho' wuz! De Lawd have mussy upon us, praise his Holy Name!"

Very obviously Harriet had sprained her ankle while looking at the old man instead of watching the path, and the hot fomentation had reduced the swelling. She is not the first person to hear spirit voices in his or her own vagrant imaginings.

On another occasion, Aunt Harriet's finger swelled up "as big as a corn cob." She at first supposed the swelling to be due to a felon. She went to old Uncle Julius Lutterloh, who told her that someone had tricked [conjured] her. "My Lawd!" she exclaimed, "how did they fix my finger?" He explained that it was done while in the act of shaking hands. "Doctor" Julius opened the finger with a sharp knife and showed Harriet two seeds at the bottom of the incision. He instructed her to put a poultice of red onions on the wound over night, and in the morning the seeds would come out. She was then to put the two seeds in a skillet, on the right hand side of the fire-place, in a pint of water, and let them simmer nine mornings, and on the ninth morning she was to let all the water simmer out, and when the last drop should have gone, the one that put the seeds in her hand was to go out of this world! Harriet, however, did not pursue the treatment to the bitter end. The seeds, once extracted, she put into a small phial, which she corked up tightly and put carefully away in her bureau drawer. One morning she went to look at them, and one of them was gone. Shortly afterwards the other disappeared. Aunt Harriet has a theory that she had been tricked by a woman of whom her husband of that time was unduly fond, and that the faithless husband had returned the seeds to their original owner. A part of the scheme of conjuration is that the conjure doctor can remove the spell and put it back upon the one who laid it. I was unable to learn, however, of any instance where this extreme penalty had been insisted upon.

Source: Adapted from "Superstitions and Folk-Lore of the South," Charles W. Chestnutt, Modern Culture, May 1901. August 2, 2008. Available online at http://www.online-literature.com/charles-chesnutt/conjure-woman/11/.

The Stolen Voice

The following narrative provides insight into the ways in which conjure doctors, the practitioners of supernatural medicine in traditional African American communities, diagnose and treat those illnesses believed to be caused by magical assaults. The tale of "The Stolen Voice" provides evidence of the practice of putting the spell "back on the one who laid it," as mentioned in "Aunt Harriet." Charles W. Chesnutt (1858–1932), African American author and social activist, wrote The Conjure Woman *(1899) and* The House Behind The Cedars *(1900). He is considered a pioneer in writing on racial themes.*

An interesting conjure story, which I heard, involves the fate of a lost voice. A certain woman's lover was enticed away by another woman, who sang very sweetly, and who, the jilted one suspected, had told lies about her. Having decided upon the method of punishment for this wickedness, the injured woman watched the other closely, in order to find a suitable opportunity for carrying out her purpose; but in vain, for the fortunate one, knowing of her enmity, would never speak to her or remain near her.

One day the jilted woman plucked a red rose from her garden, and hid herself in the bushes near her rival's cabin. Very soon an old woman came by, who was accosted by the woman in hiding, and requested to hand the red rose to the woman of the house. The old woman, suspecting no evil, took the rose and approached the house, the other woman following her closely, but keeping herself always out of sight.

When the old woman, having reached the door and called out the mistress of the house, delivered the rose as requested, the recipient thanked the giver in a loud voice, knowing the old woman to be somewhat deaf. At the moment she spoke, the woman in hiding reached up and caught her rival's voice, and clasping it tightly in her right hand, escaped unseen, to her own cabin.

At the same instant the afflicted woman missed her voice, and felt a sharp pain shoot through her left arm, just below the elbow. She at first suspected the old woman of having tricked [conjured] her through the medium of the red rose, but was subsequently informed by a conjure doctor that her voice had been stolen, and that the old woman was innocent. For the pain he gave her a bottle of medicine, of which nine drops were to be applied three times a day, and rubbed in with the first two fingers of the right hand, care being taken not to let any other part of the hand touch the arm, as this would render the medicine useless.

By the aid of a mirror, in which he called up her image, the conjure doctor ascertained who was the guilty person. He sought her out and charged her with the crime which she promptly denied. Being pressed, however, she admitted her guilt. The doctor insisted upon immediate restitution. She expressed her willingness, and at the same time her inability to comply— she had taken the voice, but did not possess the power to restore it. The conjure doctor was insistent and at once placed a spell upon her which is to remain until the lost voice is restored.

Source: Adapted from "Superstitions and Folk-Lore of the South," Charles W. Chestnutt. Modern Culture, May 1901. August 2, 2008. Available online at http://www.online-literature.com/charles-chesnutt/conjure-woman/11/.

Select Bibliography

Abrahams, Roger D., ed. *African American Folktales: Stories from Black Traditions in the New World*. New York: Pantheon, 1985.
———. *The Man-of-Words in the West Indies*. Baltimore: Johns Hopkins University Press, 1983.
Bascom, William. *African Folktales in the New World*. Bloomington: Indiana University Press, 1992.
Beckwith, Martha Warren. *Jamaica Anansi Stories. Memoirs of the American Folklore Society 17*. New York: American Folklore Society, 1924.
Courlander, Harold. *Treasury of Afro-American Folklore: The Oral Literature, Traditions, Recollections, Legends, Tales, Songs, Religious Beliefs, Customs, Sayings and Humor of Peoples of African Decent in the Americas*. New York: Crown, 1976.
Dorson, Richard. *American Negro Folktales*. Greenwich, CT: Fawcett, 1967.
Harris, Joel Chandler. *The Complete Tales of Uncle Remus*. Compiled by Richard Chase. Boston: Houghton Mifflin, 1953.
Hurston, Zora Neale. *Mules and Men*. Philadelphia: Lippincott, 1936.
Katz, William Loren. *Black Indians: A Hidden Heritage*. New York: Antheneum, 1986.
Parsons, Elsie Clews. *Folk-Lore of the Sea Islands, South Carolina. Memoirs of the American Folklore Society 16*. New York: American Folklore Society, 1923.

Index

About the Author

THOMAS A. GREEN is Associate Professor of Anthropology at Texas A&M University. His many books include *The Greenwood Library of American Folktales* (2006) and *The Greenwood Library of World Folktales* (2008).